THE MYSTERY OF
THE FORBIDDEN FOREST

THE MYSTERY OF
THE FORBIDDEN FOREST

STEVE SWANSON

ZondervanPublishingHouse
Grand Rapids, Michigan

A Division of HarperCollins*Publishers*

The Mystery of the Forbidden Forest
Copyright © 1994 by Steve Swanson

Requests for information should be addressed to:
Zondervan Publishing House
Grand Rapids, Michigan 49530

Library of Congress Cataloging-in-Publication Data

Swanson, Steve, 1932–
    The mystery of the forbidden forest / Steve Swanson.
       p.   m.—(A Penny and Chad earthkeepers adventure)
    Summary: When Chad and Penny see a heavily loaded truck enter
Wickner's Woods at night and come out empty, they decide to solve the
mystery of what's being dumped there
    ISBN 0-310-39821-5 (pbk.)
    [1. Water—Pollution—Fiction. 2. Pollution—Fiction. 3. Mystery and
detective stories.]   I. Title.   II. Series: Swanson, Steve, 1932–
Earthkeepers series.
    PZ7.S9725Mw   1994
    [Fic]—dc20
                                            94–30704
                                              CIP
                                              AC

Edited by David Lambert
Cover design by Chris Gannon
Cover illustration by Doug Knutson
Interior design by Sue Koppenol
Interior illustrations by Tim Davis

Printed in the United States of America

94 95 96 97 98 /❖DH/ 10 9 8 7 6 5 4 3 2 1

 Printed on Recycled Paper

*My sincere thanks to
Ruth Geisler, Ron Klug, and Dave Lambert
for early encouragement and help,
and to Shelley Sateren for her many
critiques and suggestions.*

Contents

An Iron Warning

"Where'd you kids get this stuff?" Ironman Kenyon asked. He picked up a few pieces of iron and steel from my bicycle trailer and turned them over as carefully as if they were made of glass.

Penny and I stood beside our bikes and looked around us at the piles of metal everywhere. Most people would call it junk, but to my friend Ironman Kenyon, each piece was useful and valuable. Behind him was the platform scale he used to weigh the metals he bought from people: copper, brass, aluminum, iron, and steel. After he bought metal, he sorted it into big steel barrels. When he had enough of them, he drove a truckful of barrels to the city to sell. And that's how he made his living—buying and selling scrap metal.

"This is real old iron, Chad, some of it," Ironman Kenyon said. "Look here." He picked up an iron casting that looked like the shell of a giant Jurassic beetle and held it toward me. "This is a gearbox cover from an old McCormick hay mower," he said, "the kind that was pulled by a team of horses."

"Wow," I said, leaning in for a closer look at the greasy metal shell. "That's old."

"See here," he said, pointing. "It's cracked. That's probably why someone threw it out."

I looked up at him. *He's like an iron and steel detective,* I thought. *He can look at a piece of metal and figure out how old it is, what it was used for, and why they threw it out. He's the Sherlock Holmes of recycled metal.*

"And this," he said, setting down the mower casting and picking up an even heavier piece of metal with a pipe sticking out of it. "This is an automatic drinking fountain from an old dairy barn." He turned it rightside up. It did look a bit like a rusty little drinking fountain. "The water came down this pipe, see." He pointed with his greasy index finger. "Down the pipe and then through this valve. When the cow put her nose down in there to drink, she pushed this thing here." He showed us by pushing down on a metal ring shaped like a five-pointed star in the middle. "When she pushed down, the valve would open and fill the cup with water so she could have a drink. They worked great when the valves didn't stick. Flooded the barn when they did."

"How do you know so much about farms?" Penny asked, smiling.

"I grew up on one," Mr. Kenyon answered. "We had cows and horses and pigs and chickens. An old-fashioned family farm. When I was little, we grew almost all our own food—except for sugar and salt and coffee. That's why I'm so big and strong," he laughed, standing up tall and touching his fists to his ears to make his arm muscles look big.

"Why did you ever leave the farm?" Penny asked.

Ironman Kenyon explained to Penny that the farm was too small to support all his brothers and sisters. That's when he started to haul metal to pick up a little extra money. It turned into his full-time work.

As he talked about his large family, I thought about my small one. Just Mom and me—and she worked all day. If I didn't have Penny to run around with after school, I'd be bored to death. Penny's family has so much money they could send her to after-school stuff like tennis clubs, but luckily she likes to hang around with me instead. I tuned back in to Ironman's story. "Oh, I did other things," he went on, "but I always hauled scrap metal for a hobby—kind of like you kids do. Pretty soon scrap collecting was taking so much time I didn't have time for other jobs," he chuckled. "But back to my first question—Where did you kids get this old stuff?"

"In Wickner's Woods," Penny said.

There was a strange silence. Mr. Kenyon got a serious look on his face.

"What's wrong?" Penny asked.

"I'm your friend, right?" Mr. Kenyon said, looking first at Penny and then at me.

"Sure," I said.

"Then, Chad and Penny, as your friend, I'm asking you not to go back to Wickner's Woods."

"But it's full of scrap metal," Penny said.

"I know it's full of scrap metal," he said. "It's been full of scrap metal for years. I've cleaned out lots of woods like that. I've hauled scrap out of almost every

11

woods for twenty-five miles in every direction—but not *Wickner's* Woods."

"Why?" Penny whispered. "Is it haunted?"

"You might say that." Mr. Kenyon didn't smile.

"What do you mean?" I asked.

"It's haunted by Al Wickner. Just do me a personal favor and stay out of his woods." There was another long pause, then he asked, "Promise?"

"I guess so," I said.

Penny said nothing.

"How about you, missy?"

Penny nodded as if she were saying yes, but she was hiding her hands behind her back. I'd seen that trick before. I looked, and sure enough—her fingers were crossed. She wasn't promising anything. *Isn't that like lying?* I wondered.

Nobody said any more about Wickner's Woods. I pushed my bike and trailer over near Mr. Kenyon's old iron scale and all three of us piled pieces of metal on the scale platform. There was almost more than the platform could hold. It was like a game where we'd lose if we made the pile tip over. When we finished, the pipes and rods and old pitchforks made the pile look like a rust-colored porcupine.

Mr. Kenyon ticked the scale's little brass weight back and forth, scribbled in a little spiral notebook, and then said, "I owe you two dollars and thirty-two cents."

His puffy brown billfold had a silver chain that was attached to his belt. He reached back and found the chain, pulled the billfold out of his back pocket, and took two bills from it. Then he reached for a coffee can he kept on top of the scale, rattling coins around in it until he had two pennies and three dimes in his hand. He changed his mind, though, threw one dime back in and came up with two nickels instead. He knew Penny and I always split every penny we earned from recycling. As he handed us the money he added, "I should pay you each ten dollars hazard pay for being in Wickner's Woods."

We just smiled.

On our way home Penny asked, "Have you ever seen Al Wickner?" She pumped her bike in time with her words.

"I don't think so," I answered. "I heard him holler from his woods once. Some kids were climbing on his rickety old fence. His *voice* sounded scary—like thunder or something."

We rode along in silence for a long time, until we were only a few blocks from my house. "No one could be as scary," Penny frowned, "as Mr. Kenyon made him sound."

"Mr. Kenyon sure didn't want us to go back."

"I think we *should* go back," Penny said as we pulled up behind my garage. "A lot of scrap metal is going to waste in those woods. It's our duty as good members of Earthkeepers."

Being members of Earthkeepers, I thought as I lifted the garage door, had taught us a lot about recycling and earth care—but besides that, while we were doing things for our Earthkeepers club, things like saving aluminum cans and cleaning road ditches, we kept getting into these adventures. I wondered if Wickner's Woods was like a forbidden forest in a mystery story. Would we be sorry if we went back in there?

"Sorry, but I can't go back to those woods," I finally said. "I promised Mr. Kenyon I wouldn't."

"Well, I didn't. Not exactly. And you didn't, either," Penny said, sounding like a lawyer, "Not really. You didn't say, 'I promise,' you said, 'I guess so.' That's not exactly a promise."

"Well, maybe I don't *want* to go back," I argued.

"What could be so bad about Mr. Wickner? Remember Mr. Strange? We found a gun in his garbage can and believed all kinds of horrible things about him. Then we met him, and he wasn't like that at all."

"So?"

"And how about Mr. Orandi? Remember how we thought he was the one who stole the golden tiger?"

"Of course I remember all that. But not everyone turns out to be nice. There are mean people in this world."

Penny didn't look convinced. "I know," she said, "but—"

"Like," I went on, "I'll bet no matter how well you got to know someone like Jack the Ripper, he wouldn't be nice. Maybe Mr. Wickner's like that."

Penny thought about that, and then didn't look so sure of herself. For once I had her. "And maybe he isn't," she finally said. "At least we ought to give him a chance."

"But not by trespassing on his land."

"We could walk up the creek and just look around. He doesn't own the creek. Nobody can own a creek. Maybe if we showed up there once in a while, we could get to know him. Be his friend."

I didn't want to go back on Mr. Wickner's land. I could still see the look on Ironman Kenyon's face when

14

we mentioned his name. "Why don't we just call Mr. Wickner," I finally said, "and ask him if we—or better yet, Earthkeepers—could go through his woods and collect the metal?"

"I guess we could do that," Penny said, twirling her French braid.

"All he could do is say no," I said. "If he gives us permission, then I wouldn't even be going against my promise."

"Let's go in and call him right now," Penny said impatiently.

We parked our bikes in the garage and went inside. The kitchen felt hot as we stepped in, but that was just because outdoors the wind still felt like the end of a long Minnesota winter. Spring wasn't here yet. It was still plenty cold.

It was the first week of March, and Penny and I had the rest of the month to map the stars in the evening sky for our science class. We planned on doing it together, maybe with Jay. The three of us were all listening to weather reports and waiting for a few warm, cloudless nights, which didn't usually go together around here. The clear nights were always the coldest.

But if March wasn't so great for star watching, it was the perfect month for metal salvage. When the winter snow melted away, it always left last summer's grass all packed down. Whatever the weeds and grass had been hiding since last May was now right in plain sight. The Highway Department knew that, too. March and April were always Adopt-A-Highway cleanup months.

"You want milk or hot chocolate or anything?" I asked Penny as we pulled off our jackets.

"No thanks. Let's make the call and then I have to go home."

I pulled out the phone book to look up Wickner's number. "You do the talking," I said. "You sound nicer on the phone. I'll go upstairs and listen on the extension."

I lifted up the phone as Penny was still dialing. The sound seemed magnified in the upstairs phone.

Someone answered. "Yeah?"

"Hello," Penny said in an almost-too-sweet voice. "Is this Mr. Wickner?"

"Yes it is," he answered gruffly. "What do you want?"

"This is Penelope Palmer. I'm a member of Earth-keepers, and we were wondering if we could have some of the scrap metal in your woods for recycling."

"No, you can't. I don't want you or anyone else in my woods. You trespass on my property, you'll be sorry, you understand?"

"Yes sir," Penny said in what sounded like a scared voice.

"Good," he said and hung up. The receiver clicked loud and hard.

I ran downstairs. Penny was sitting there holding the buzzing phone a foot in front of her nose. "What a mean old buzzard," she said, shaking the phone in her fist. From upstairs she had sounded scared. Now she looked mad.

"Mr. Kenyon was right," I finally said. "We should stay away from him."

"What would it hurt for us to clean up that metal? It's not doing him any good. Maybe the old buzzard doesn't want us in his woods because he's hiding something."

"What?"

"I don't know," Penny said, her voice strong and determined now, "but I'm going to find out."

Penny is dead-cat curious. Whenever she smells a mystery, you can't hold her back.

"Remember, I promised," I reminded her.

"Well, *I* didn't," she said.

After school the next day, Penny said she was going exploring in Wickner's Woods.

"I'm not," I said.

"Then I'll find someone else. Jay would go."

It makes me mad when she gets like this. She'd probably go alone if no one would go with her, she's so stubborn. "That's not fair. You heard me promise Mr. Kenyon."

"Chad," she said, "there's something suspicious going on in those woods. Or else why's Mr. Wickner so worried that someone might snoop around?"

"I don't know," I said, shaking my head.

"Maybe he's just a buzzard," Penny said. She'd called him a buzzard yesterday, too. Maybe that was going to be her name for him.

I laughed. "Yesterday you said he might be nice!"

"I said that *before* we called him on the phone!"

"After what we heard," I said, "I wouldn't snoop there—and neither should you."

Penny flashed one of her sly smiles and said, "We haven't had a good adventure yet this spring."

"We've been lucky so far," I said. "Let's keep it that way."

I should have listened to my own advice, I thought at dusk that day, as we rode our mountain bikes toward Wickner's Woods. *At least pedaling past his place won't be breaking any promises. It won't hurt just to ride by and have a look.*

Famous last words.

At the edge of town, the paved road suddenly became a gravel road. A few small houses stood in a row on one side of the road, with the woods on the other. A rusty old barbed-wire fence with rotten posts sagged and swayed around the edge of Mr. Wickner's property. Most of the posts were broken off right at ground level, with just the wire holding them up. Obviously, no horses or cows were kept in by that fence.

A U-Rent truck drove by us slowly, then turned in at Mr. Wickner's long driveway and disappeared into the trees. Although it was almost dark, the truck lights were turned off when he entered the driveway.

You couldn't see any of Mr. Wickner's buildings from the road. In fact, you couldn't even tell if there *were* any buildings. I remembered Mom once calling Wickner's place "an old farm." I guess most of the old farms around here had a woods like that. Besides, Ironman Kenyon said the metal we found in the woods was from old farm machines and equipment.

As if in answer to my wondering, I heard an engine start up. It had the same rattle as a diesel engine in an eighteen-wheeler makes. I watched for black smoke at the tops of the trees.

"What is that?" Penny asked.

"Has to be a truck or a tractor."

"Would he be farming after dark?" Penny asked.

"A lot of farmers do at harvest time," I answered.

"This isn't harvest time; this is March," she scoffed. "Besides, farmers don't drive around in U-Rent trucks. They have their own trucks."

"Let's just get out of here," I said. It was getting darker, Mr. Kenyon had warned us, and I had made a promise.

"I'm going up to the top of his hill to take a look."

"No you're not," I said, trying to make my voice sound like our school principal.

"You going to stop me?" she whispered with a smile.

This was getting serious. Mr. Wickner himself had specifically warned us to stay away. Now Penny wanted to go in. Should I go with her? Should I break my promise? Should I try to keep her out?

Who're you trying to kid? I thought. *She's never changed her mind about anything, so there's no chance you're going to talk her out of this. You can go in with her, or you can let her go in alone.* I finally decided I'd better go in with her. I think I was more scared than she was, but two of us going somehow seemed better than one. *You're breaking a promise to a friend,* I told myself, and I felt pretty bad about it.

Still, promise or no promise, I wasn't going to let her go in there alone. I made Penny promise *me* something, though. "I'll go with you," I said, "if you promise to go just to the top of the hill and take a quick look."

"Good," Penny said. "Let's hide our bikes here in the ditch and then run for it."

We pushed our bikes down through the ditch and up behind some bushes near the fence. We could barely see in the settling darkness, but we soon found a place where the fence posts were tipped almost to the ground. We stepped over the wires easily and then ran toward the top of the hill.

When we got to the top, we stopped, puffing. The woods were thinner here and we could now see between the trees. Below us we saw Mr. Wickner's farmstead, a terribly run-down place. A half-dozen gray, sagging buildings stood in a circle around an overgrown roadway that made a loop at the end of his long lane. On the far end of the circle the small white wooden house needed a paint job pretty bad. The building nearest the house was a sagging old barn with a gaping doorway on the second floor—the kind of doorway they're always loading hay through in old western movies. Looked like the door was missing, though—which made the barn look like a turtle with its mouth open.

I looked for the U-Rent truck, but didn't spot it at first. Finally I saw it between the house and the old barn. The truck was facing us, and the tractor we'd heard was behind it, as if they were using the loading bucket on the tractor to unload something from the truck.

"Over there," I pointed.

"I see it," Penny whispered. "Wonder what they're doing."

"Looks like they may be loading or unloading something," I whispered back.

"Do you suppose Wickner's packing up and moving?" Penny whispered. "That's what most people do with U-Rent trucks."

"Maybe. Let's watch and see if they're loading or *un*loading the truck."

We never got a chance to watch anything. The sound came from nearby and was unmistakable: A dog, a snarling angry dog—and from the sound of it, a big dog. It didn't bark—just snarled.

I reached for Penny's hand and discovered that she was also reaching for mine. We held hands and backed away slowly. "Easy boy," I said, as gently as my trembling voice would let me.

We backed halfway down the hill, feeling our way behind ourselves with our sneakers. Taking baby steps, we turned to look over our shoulders in quick glances, hoping not to trip over anything and be pounced on and eaten alive by the snarling dog.

It didn't sound like the dog had moved—but we could still hear it snarling even though we were halfway to the fence. We still had about fifty feet to go when Penny whispered urgently, "Let's run for it."

We turned and tried to run. We had forgotten to let go of each other's hand and turned in instead of out, crashing together nose to nose. We got tangled and almost fell over each other but wouldn't let go, either. When we finally got our backs to the hill, we ran for the fence. We were still hand in hand—running and stumbling—heading for the low spot in the fence as fast as we could run.

The dog's snarl turned to a bark and started to get closer. The dog was running, too. I prayed a quick prayer, *Please don't let that dog get us,* then immediately felt guilty and added, *and forgive me for breaking my promise.*

We finally reached the fence and dived over, rolling into the damp grass in the ditch. We let go of each other's hands now and scrambled up into a run. We headed across the road and into the front yard of one of the houses. We hid behind a front yard tree and watched to see if the dog would come across the road after us.

He didn't cross the fence, but we could hear him, over by our bikes, sniffing.

It got real quiet. The sky darkened, and the street joined it. There were no street lights. We stared into the darkness, trying to tell for sure whether the dog had gone back over the hill or not. We stood there for at least five minutes, not saying a word, listening for any sound.

"Let's see if we can get to our bikes," I whispered.

We sneaked across the road, picked up our bikes, and rolled them quickly up onto the asphalt. Just to get farther from the dog, we wheeled our bikes into the ditch on the other side of the road and up onto the grassy yard. There was no sidewalk, so we just began walking our bikes toward home.

"I wish we could watch his place from a helicopter or a hot-air balloon," Penny whispered. "Someplace way up high and safe."

"We need a tower with a ladder we could pull up," I whispered back. "You think that dog could climb ladders?"

"We don't have to whisper anymore," Penny said out loud.

"I think it eats legs," I said.

"Were you scared?" Penny asked.

"Weren't you?" I said, and we both laughed in relief. Yeah, we'd been scared. If it had been me and Jay, instead of me and Penny, who got chased by the dog, we'd have never admitted how scared we were.

When we got home, Mom was waiting in the kitchen. Penny leaned against the wall just inside the door and I sank into a chair.

"Your mother just called, Penelope, wondering where you were." Mom ended her sentence with a loving little pat to Penny's cheek. Always one to be fair, Mom then walked over to me, put a hand on each of my cheeks, and kissed me on top of the head.

"We were out on the edge of town, and it got dark on us," I said.

"We had to walk our bikes back," Penny added.

I decided not to tell her about Mr. Wickner, or his woods, or his dog—at least not right now. No sense making her worried. It was done with, and I had no intentions of going back there. Mr. Kenyon was right.

"By the way," Mom said, "while you and Penelope are both here. . . . I talked to Emma Furrow at church last week."

"Who's Emma Furrow?" I asked.

"I don't think you know her. She's an older woman. A widow. Her husband died a couple of years ago. Anyway, the reason I mention it is this: Her husband's hobby was welding."

"So?"

"So their garage is full of metal, and she says you Earthkeepers can have it."

"Wow," Penny and I both said.

"Where does she live?" I asked.

"Out on the edge of town. It's a darling little house. Everything in it is old. She even has a little wood stove in her living room. She needs someone to climb up on her roof and run a brush down her chimney. Do you think you could do that when you go out to get the metal?"

"Sure," Penny said.

"I wouldn't let you risk it," Mom said, "but she says the roof is almost flat. She cleaned the chimney herself until last year."

"Where is this house?" Penny asked.

"You can look up the address in the phone book. You can't miss it, though. It's a white frame house with green trim, and it's right across the road from Wickner's Woods."

We went out to Emma Furrow's house right after school the next day. We parked our bikes near the road in front of her house and turned to look at Wickner's Woods.

"Doesn't look so scary in the daylight," I said.

"Stupid dog," Penny said, straining her eyes as if she were trying to see right through the woods.

"I hope that dog's been eaten by ETs from Mars," I laughed.

"This house is like an answer to prayer," Penny said.

"I know. And we're even invited to go up on the roof."

"We can watch everything that goes on at the Wickner place," Penny said eagerly. "But how long can we make a chimney-cleaning job last?"

"A couple of days, at least," I said, "if we work it right."

We knocked on the door and were invited in by a tiny old lady. Penny and I stood quietly just inside the door. *Mom was right,* I thought, as I looked around. *Everything is old—even Mrs. Furrow. Not ancient, though, just older.* Her single gray braid went halfway down to her waist. Hair and all, she couldn't have weighed even a hundred pounds—less than Penny weighed, I guessed.

Mrs. Furrow wore a dress and an apron. When my eyes got to her feet, they did a double take. She saw me staring at her expensive Demetrius running shoes.

"Like my shoes?" she asked. "I get them free. My son owns a sporting-goods store in Des Moines. He tells me to help myself to fancy sweat suits and rain gear and such. I can't wear that sort of clothes—but I can wear the shoes. Boy, I really like these shoes!" She tapped her feet on the floor in a little dance, surprising me. "So you're Penny and Chad," she finally said "Well, well. Penny and Chad. And you can call me Emm. I hate 'Emma'."

We all laughed. I couldn't help myself. She hadn't said anything all that funny—she just had a great laugh. Deep and rich. Made you want to laugh along.

"In the olden days, they used to call a frown a furrowed brow." She demonstrated. "But that must not be where I got my name—I don't frown much."

We all laughed again.

"Mom said you might have some metal for recycling," I said.

"*Some* metal! I have a whole garage full! My husband brought home every piece of stray metal he could find. Then he made things out of it. Most of them were useless—except for that stool over there. See that stool? It's made out of an old cast-iron tractor seat. And that coat rack over there," she pointed at a stand near the door. "See that? He made that out of the frame of an old horse-drawn buggy. I keep that there by the door because it reminds me of him. He was a bit buggy, too."

Penny laughed so hard her eyes watered. She wiped them with the back of her hand, then walked over and looked at the stool. "It's beautiful," she said, running her fingers over the intricate castings.

"Try it," Mrs. Furrow suggested. "It's really quite comfortable."

Penny sat down carefully, and as she wiggled around on the seat she said, "It's cool—a cool stool—both ways."

Emma Furrow laughed until *she* nearly cried. "That stool feels great on a hot summer's day," she said, raising and lowering her eyebrows like Groucho Marx.

She led us through the house, into the kitchen, and out the back door. We walked along a winding path made from stone slabs and stopped in front of the garage door. She reached down and pulled on the handle, raising the door. "See? Just look at that."

Penny and I just stood there and stared, our mouths hanging open. The garage was jammed full of metal. Some of it was sorted—like rods and lengths of angle iron sticking out of metal pails. Most of it, though, was just piled in corners and under the workbench.

"Don't you want to keep any of it?" I asked.

"I gave the longer and larger pieces of metal to a couple of his welding friends," she said. "The rest of this stuff is just junk. They didn't want it and neither do I. Until I talked to your mother," she nodded at me, "I couldn't imagine what I was going do with it. You'd be doing me a great favor by hauling it away."

"There's a lot of old metal lying around in Wickner's Woods, too," Penny said, pointing down Mrs. Furrow's dirt driveway and across the road, "but he won't let us have *any* of it."

"Doesn't surprise me," Mrs. Furrow said. "Wickner's a strange man. Sour. Sour as a green lemon. He's the one who should be named Furrow."

I wanted to hear more about Mr. Wickner—and I was sure Penny did, too—but we didn't dare seem too curious. Mrs. Furrow lived right across the road. Maybe she had seen something going on over there. But we had to wait for the right time to ask. I changed the subject: "Mom also said you'd like your chimney cleaned."

"I sure would. It's not that altogether hard to do. I did it myself for years. The doctor told me I had to quit climbing around, that's all. I have osteoporosis, and he said I might fall and break something important—like my head."

"We'll be glad to clean your chimney for you," Penny said, smiling. I wondered if she knew what osteoporosis was. I didn't.

"I'd pay you."

"You don't have to," I said. "Especially if you're going to give us all that metal."

"I wish all kids were as nice as you two," Mrs. Furrow said.

She turned then and pointed to the wall. "The ladder's hanging on the side of the garage," she said, "just on the other side of that wall. The chimney brush is around here somewhere." She rummaged around next to the workbench and finally came up with several lengths of rod and a stout brush with thick plastic bristles. It looked like a porcupine. "You just screw the brush on the end of one of these rods, like this," she said, showing us. "Then you screw the rods together, then run the brush up and down inside the pipe." She demonstrated. "Nothing to it."

I could see there was nothing to it. I could see that the whole operation wouldn't take more than twenty minutes. Unfortunately. So much for our several days on her roof, cleaning the chimney. So much for our setting up a watch on Wickner's Woods.

"I won't use my wood stove any more this spring, so you could do it anytime. Right now if you wanted."

"We don't have much time right now," I said. Penny gave me a puzzled look. "We just have enough time to set the ladder up and have a quick look."

Mrs. Furrow raised her eyebrows. "Once you get the ladder set up, you might just as well do the chimney. Won't take that long."

"I'd rather clean the chimney when we have more time—in case there's some problem or some hitch."

"Chad, we—" Penny started to object.

I cut her off. "We just have time for a quick look," I said firmly. "I want to make sure we have enough time to do the job right."

"The chimney I want cleaned is the little silver one on this end of the house," she said, pointing, "not the big brick one down there. You put up the ladder and have your look then," Mrs. Furrow said. "While you're doing that, I'll go in and fix a bag of sugar cookies that you can take with you."

"Great," Penny said.

When we were up on the roof, Penny asked, "Why did you say we haven't much time? I thought we had all afternoon."

"Because we have to spend the rest of the afternoon figuring out how we can stretch this little twenty-minute chimney-cleaning job into several afternoons."

"Oh," Penny said, understanding instantly.

We walked down the ridge toward the silver chimney. Mrs. Furrow's roof was one of the flattest roofs I had ever been on. "Hurry," I said to Penny. "We don't have much time."

"Thanks to you," Penny said, elbowing me. She elbowed me so hard I had to step off the ridge to catch my balance.

"Sorry."

"Anyway, how much can we see from here?" I asked. We both turned and looked toward the Wickner place.

"Not much from this end of the house," Penny said. "How about down by her *big* chimney?"

We turned and walked back down the ridge of the roof and stood by what must have been a fireplace chimney. It came up the outside wall of her house and went past the ridge, extending about six feet above the roof—a foot or so over our heads.

"You can see down his lane from here," Penny pointed. "You can even see part of his yard."

"If this roof were just a little higher, we could see his *whole* yard."

"Maybe from the top of the chimney," Penny said. "Put your knee against the chimney and let me use it for a step. I'm climbing up."

34

She was *what?* "No you're not," I insisted.

"You keep telling me what to do. Cut it out."

"But, Penny, you could—"

"Just put your knee over here."

I sighed and went down on one knee. I put the other one against the chimney and held on to the corners of the chimney for balance. Penny put one foot on my knee and a hand on top of my head and then stood up on my knee. From there she could boost herself up onto the top of the chimney. When she was up there and on her knees, she simply stood up.

"You be careful," I said.

"You worry too much," Penny said.

"What can you see?"

"Everything. His whole yard."

"What are you doing up there?" shouted a voice from below. It was Mrs. Furrow. She was standing on the front yard looking up at us. Our bag of cookies was in her hand.

"I'm just seeing how far I can see from up here!" Penny shouted back.

"How far *can* you see?"

"China!" Penny answered. We all laughed so hard that Penny almost lost her balance. She went down to her knees again and then slid herself down onto *my* knee and back onto the roof.

"We'd better go down," I whispered.

When we were halfway back down the ladder, Penny whispered, "We didn't even look at the silver chimney."

"Tomorrow," I whispered back.

"You're some climber," Mrs. Furrow said to Penny as we were hanging the ladder back on its nails. She patted Penny's cheek just like my mom does. There just must be something about Penny's cheek.

"I'm sorry if my being up there frightened you, Mrs. Furrow," Penny said.

"I wasn't frightened," she said. "You didn't seem to be, so I wasn't. And please call me Emm. You remind me of myself when I was your age. Always up in trees or on roofs. I liked to be up in the air."

"I do, too," Penny said.

"Well, here are your cookies. Think you can manage to share them?"

"I'm sure we can, Mrs.—" Penny caught herself. "I mean, Emm."

"Good. Who gets to hold the bag?"

"Doesn't matter," I said.

"All right, then, I'll give them to Penny. If she can stand on top of a chimney, she should be able to ride a bike with one hand."

"I sure can," Penny said. "We'll be eating cookies all the way home."

"Save a couple for your mother, Chad. She always buys my sugar cookies at the church's Fall Bazaar."

"I'll make sure he does," Penny said, laughing.

"*Now* who's bossing whom around?" I said.

"We'll be back tomorrow after school," Penny said.

"We'll clean your chimney and then sort out some of the metal," I added.

"Thanks. I'll look for you."

A Brush with the Stars

Penny and I went back to Mrs. Furrow's the next day—but not until about 5:00. It was hard not to go right after school, but we decided that if we went later, toward sunset, we'd be more likely to see some action over at Wickner's.

"Hi, Penny. Hi, Chad," Mrs. Furrow shouted from her porch as we leaned our bikes against her tree. "I thought you'd come right after school."

"We decided to wait a while," Penny said. Mrs. Furrow didn't ask us why and we didn't want to tell her.

"Maybe we could look at the scrap metal first," I said, "then go up on the roof after that." I wanted it to be as dark as possible when we went up on the roof.

"Sure," Mrs. Furrow said. "But first we'll have to spend a few minutes in the kitchen," she said in an I've-got-a-secret voice.

"Why?" Penny asked. "What's going on?"

"What's going on, is what's going on the table. I made a batch of chocolate-chip cookies this afternoon, and bought a half-gallon of milk to go with them."

"Yum," Penny and I both said together—then said "Jinx" together, then pulled little fingers.

"We used to do that when I was young," Mrs. Furrow said. "When we had our fingers locked good and tight, we'd recite a poem:

> *Needles, pins,*
> *Triplets, twins,*
> *When a girl marries*
> *Her troubles begin.*

"Then we'd pull little fingers until one person gave up and let her finger straighten out."

"Let's try it," Penny said to me.

We locked our fingers together again. "How does it go?" I asked.

Mrs. Furrow got us started: "Needles, pins . . ."

We pulled as hard as we could. Penny won, just because she's more stubborn.

"Did you ever bite down on your fingernail and then pull?" Mrs. Furrow asked.

Penny shook her head.

"Try it," Mrs. Furrow said with a strange smile.

We did. "Ow!" we both shouted, shaking out our tingling fingers.

"Isn't that fun?" she laughed.

"You have a weird idea of fun," Penny chuckled.

We sat and talked and ate cookies for about ten minutes. After that it got quiet. "Is it true?" Penny finally asked Mrs. Furrow.

"Is what true, child?"

"Is it true," Penny asked, "what it says in the poem: 'When a girl marries, her troubles begin'?"

"Not for me, it wasn't true," Mrs. Furrow said. "Being married to Bill was the nicest thing that ever happened to me."

"My mom might think it's true," I said softly.

"I doubt that," Mrs. Furrow said. "At least not when she was first married. I remember your father, Chad. He had his faults. All men do. But he was a good person."

All I could manage was half a smile. I wished more people would say nice things about my father. I wanted to have some good feelings about him.

Penny could see things were getting too personal. "Out to the garage," she said, jumping up from the kitchen table and running for the door. "And thanks for the cookies and milk." She stopped at the door and waited for me.

"I've been making cookies like that for fifty years," Mrs. Furrow said as we walked out the door. "First my children, then my grandchildren, now you."

In the garage, Penny and I just walked around among all the scrap metal with our eyes wide. Most of it was iron and steel, but there were odds and ends of other metals too: brass, copper, and aluminum.

"There's a *fortune* here," I whispered, not wanting Mrs. Furrow to hear.

"We're not out to make a fortune," Penny whispered back. "Besides, how are we going to haul it?"

"There's too much for my little bicycle trailer," I said. "We need a pickup truck or big trailer someone can pull with a car."

41

"We could rent a trailer," Penny said.

"Rent a trailer," I said as if a light had just gone on in my brain. "Maybe if we went down to the rental place, we could find out who's been using that U-Rent truck."

"The one going in and out of Wickner's Woods," Penny said.

"Right. Let's go down to U-Rent after school tomorrow," I said.

"Great. But right now, let's get up on that roof."

We took the ladder off the wall and gathered the parts of the chimney brush. Before we went up on the roof, we screwed all the rods of the chimney brush together, then carried the ladder from the garage to the back of the house. Together we leaned it up against the rain gutter on the roof. Penny climbed up first, then I handed her the long-handled chimney brush.

"You two be careful up there," Mrs. Furrow warned.

"It's an easy roof," I said.

"He fell off an easier roof than this," Penny shouted down to Mrs. Furrow. "He broke his leg, too." Penny smiled a sly smile my way.

"Did you really?" Mrs. Furrow looked worried.

"I *fell*," I said extra loudly, glaring at Penny, "because someone was *shooting* at me."

"Really? You'll have to tell me all about that when you come down. Maybe you could tell me about it while I fix some supper for us all. What would you say to that?"

"We'd have to call home,'" I shouted, climbing up onto the roof.

"I'll make the calls while you're cleaning the chimney," she shouted back.

Penny and I went over and hoisted the long brush straight up over the silver chimney and then pushed it down in. I was right. Cleaning the chimney took only about twenty minutes. It wasn't even dark yet, and we had no excuse to stay on the roof.

"Let's leave the brush up here," I suggested.

"Why?" Penny asked, as if that was the stupidest thing she'd ever heard.

"It'll work like this," I said in a tone of voice to match hers, a voice that said, *When you hear my idea you won't think it's so stupid.* "After supper I'll say, 'Oh, phooey, I forgot the brush on the roof.' Then we'll have an excuse to come back up here after dark and have another look."

"Great idea," Penny said, slugging my shoulder.

We had a neat supper: grilled cheese sandwiches, chicken-noodle soup, and one of our favorites, PBC—Peanut Butter Celery—celery sticks with peanut butter smeared in the valleys. Before we started, Mrs. Furrow prayed, "I thank you God, as always, for this food, and a special thanks for my two young friends here who are bringing freshness and joy into my life."

Once we started eating, and Mrs. Furrow saw how Penny and I crunched our celery at each other, she joined us. Pretty soon all three of us were crunching peanut-butter celery in each other's faces and laughing like chipmunks.

When it was time to go home, I said, "Oh. You know what? We forgot the chimney broom on the roof."

"Leave it there," Mrs. Furrow said. "Come back another afternoon and get it down."

"We don't need an excuse to come back," Penny smiled.

"How nice of you to say that," Mrs. Furrow said, patting Penny on the cheek again.

"We'll get the brush now," I said, "then it'll be done."

Up on the roof again, Penny and I tried to focus our eyes on Wickner's place. There was no sound or movement at all and no lights.

"Nothing going on tonight," I said.

"Whatever he's doing over there," Penny added, "it doesn't go on every night. Just sometimes."

Neither of us said anything for awhile. For the first time, I noticed what was around us. Penny must have noticed, too. "It's really pretty up here at night," she said, leaning back and looking over her head. "Look at that sky."

"And those stars," I added. The evening stars were just appearing.

"Stars!" we both shouted at exactly the same moment. We were so excited that neither of us said "Jinx."

"Of course," Penny said.

"We'll do our map of the stars from this very roof." Then I added, "If she'll let us."

"We can spend as many nights as we like up here," Penny said, her eyes sparkling in the half-darkness.

"If she'll let us," I added again.

"Of course she'll let us," Penny said. "She loves having us here."

"Of course you can!" Mrs. Furrow almost shouted when we were back in her kitchen telling her about our science project. "Do you know why the stars are so bright from my roof?"

"No,' Penny said.

"Why?" I asked.

"Because it's darker here, and you can see better. We have no street lights out here."

We all walked out the back door and looked up to the sky. Mrs. Furrow snapped off the backyard light as we walked out. When our eyes got used to the darkness, we looked up. There were only a few puffy clouds above us, and the air was getting nippy.

"It's beautiful," I said.

"God is good," Mrs. Furrow said. "God is good to send me such nice young friends."

"We'd better get home before we freeze," Penny said.

"Call me and let me know what nights you want to stargaze," Mrs. Furrow said. "If you call by noon, I can have cookies baked."

"You don't need to make cookies every time we come," Penny protested.

"Of course I do," Mrs. Furrow said. "There's not a thing in this world I'd rather do."

5 A Road Not Taken

The next afternoon, right from school, Penny and I went down to U-Rent Trucks and Trailers and looked around. There were several sizes of trailers and several sizes of trucks.

"Can you figure out which size truck we saw at Wickner's Woods?" I asked Penny.

"That size, I think," she said, pointing. "Not sure, though."

"Think they'd give us names of people who rented their trucks?" I asked.

"Nah. Even if they did, there are so many trucks. How would we know which one?"

"I guess we'd have to follow it or mark it or something."

"Well, let's do what we came here for," Penny said, walking from trailer to trailer. "Let's see how much it costs to rent a trailer." After she had looked at several, she asked, "How big a one do we need?"

"If we get a trailer big enough to haul all that metal in one load," I said, "it would be too heavy for Mom's car."

"Maybe this size, then." Penny walked over to a medium-sized trailer and kicked the tire.

"Maybe so."

We went inside and told the man we wanted to rent a trailer.

"You need a car to pull a trailer," he smiled.

"We have a car," Penny said.

"You also need someone with a driver's license to drive the car."

When he saw we were serious, he opened a spiral book on the counter and gave us the prices for different-sized trailers for a week, a day, and a half-day.

We decided that if we could haul everything in a half-day, we'd still have plenty left over from what we'd make on the scrap. We walked out of the rental office and jumped on our bikes.

"Let's ride out to Ironman Kenyon's," I said. "Let's make sure he'll buy all that stuff from us."

When we got to Mr. Kenyon's scrap yard, he was running his metal baler. The engine sounded like the one we heard in Wickner's Woods. A diesel. It was idling easily, making dark puffs of exhaust, some of them perfect circles like smoke rings, as he loaded the big hopper. With his loader, he dumped in a washing machine and some stovepipe and steel chair legs, empty metal pails, a metal ironing board, and a dozen other kinds of tin and lightweight metal.

He pulled a lever and the engine began to snarl like a giant-sized version of Mr. Wickner's dog. A flap bigger than our dining-room table came down onto and then into the hopper, crunching everything flat. Then one side of the hopper moved toward the other side, squishing everything into a long square tube. Finally a plunger pushed into the tube, squeezing everything into a cube at one end. It was kind of like three hands squeezing a bundle of aluminum foil into a corner.

When all the arms in the crusher had pulled back to where they started, all that was left of all that hopper full of metal was a cube about half the size of a garbage can. Mr. Kenyon pulled another lever, and the cube flipped out into a chute.

Both Penny and I were fascinated. We stared at the little bale, made of all that stuff. "Look," Penny shouted over the noise of the still-rumbling engine, pointing. "There's the ironing board."

"What's left of it," I laughed.

"Neat," Penny shouted as she watched, holding her ears. The engine was loud and when the metal crunched, it cried and squeaked like it was alive.

When he had loaded the hopper three more times and crushed three bales, Mr. Kenyon shut down the machine.

"Wow!" Penny shouted at him.

He pulled little ear plugs out of his ears and said to her, "What?"

I said, "wow!"

"Quite a machine, isn't it," he said. "When I get a truckload of bales, I haul them to the city. I can get a heavy load on the truck when it's baled like that."

"Speaking of loads," Penny said, "We have a big load for you."

"That's good news," he said. "Where is it?"

"In Emma Furrow's garage. It was her husband's welding metal."

"Bill Furrow? I knew him. I went to high school with one of his kids. After Bill retired, he was always out here digging around for odd pieces of metal. He was forever welding something together. How much metal is there?"

"A whole garage full. Way too much for Chad's little trailer," Penny said.

"We were going to rent a trailer and let my mom pull it out here with her car."

"No need for that," Mr. Kenyon said. "I have extra pickup trucks here. When someone junks an old pickup that still runs, I use it until it quits. I can park one of my old pickups right in front of Emma's garage door, and you two can take as long as you want to load it. When it's full, all you have to do is call me. I'll come and drive it over the scale at the Farmers' Elevator and have it weighed."

"That sounds great," Penny shouted. "That would be a lot easier."

"Sure would," I said.

We rode our bikes back along the road until we came to the edge of town. We agreed to meet at my house about 7:00 for our first night of stargazing from Emma Furrow's roof.

We got to Mrs. Furrow's about 7:15. She had brownies and milk ready for us. "Not quite dark yet," she said. As we were eating and talking, I heard a truck outside. Penny jumped up and ran to the front window. "Just a pickup," she said. "Went right on by."

"What's so interesting about trucks? Half the traffic out here is trucks."

"Nothing," Penny said.

But I thought maybe the time had come to tell Mrs. Furrow what we were up to. After all, she lived right here, across from Wickner's driveway. Maybe she could help. I was sure we could trust her.

"When we were in Wickner's woods last week," I said, "we saw a U-Rent truck drive in. Someone on a tractor, maybe Mr. Wickner, was unloading something from the truck."

"You know, I've wondered about that," she said thoughtfully. "Every week or so a truck like that goes in loaded and comes out empty."

"How could you tell when it was loaded and when it was empty?" Penny asked.

"When trucks are loaded," I answered, before Mrs. Furrow could, "they hang low in back." I loved it when I knew something Penny didn't.

"Oh, of course," Penny said. "So—what do you suppose he's up to over there?"

"Hard to figure him," Mrs. Furrow said. "He's always into something—and usually on the very edge of illegal."

"Like what?" Penny asked.

"Oh, like, about ten years ago he put all his farmland in the soil bank, then planted it in alfalfa. That would have been okay if he hadn't cut it—but he did, and then sold all the hay. Some of the neighbors reported him. He traps beaver and muskrat out of season, too, and he has been known to put gill nets in the creek, during spawning time, to catch illegal fish just when they should be going up the creek to lay eggs."

"We kind of thought he was that way," Penny said.

51

"That's why we wanted to watch from your roof—" I began the sentence.

"While we were mapping the stars," Penny finished.

"Well, you watch all you like. But you'll have to promise me one thing."

"Not to fall?" Penny snorted, elbowing me.

"No," Mrs. Furrow chuckled. "Something even better. You'll have to promise that if things get interesting—you'll let me know. I don't want to miss any of the intrigue."

Out in back, we lifted the ladder off the garage wall and leaned it against the back of the roof. I had a small backpack with our notebooks, a star-and-constellation map, and a flashlight in it. I slipped the pack on my back while Penny started up the ladder. But she got only halfway up and then came back down.

"There's a stepladder in the garage, isn't there?" she asked.

"I think so. What do we need that for?"

"Suppose something happens over at Wickner's, and we need to see better. I'm not climbing up on that chimney at night."

"Why a stepladder?"

"Lean it against the chimney. Stand on the ladder, not the chimney."

"Good thinking."

We went back to the garage and pulled out the stepladder. Penny climbed the big ladder first and stood on the roof. I pushed the stepladder up ahead of me, and when it was high enough, she pulled it up. Before I could even get to the top of the ladder, she had carried the stepladder to the end of the house, leaned it against the chimney, and was up on it, peering at Wickner's buildings.

"Nothing going on there," she said. "The yard light's on, but nothing's happening."

"Let's just look at stars for awhile," I said. "We have to do that, too."

We watched the stars for about a half hour. We'd look at the sky, then snap on the flashlight to study the map of constellations, then go back to looking at the stars again. We easily found the Big Dipper and from that, the North Star. We found Orion the Hunter—well, at least his belt, and then his knife, but we had a hard time with the rest of his body. Cassiopeia, the big W, was easy, too. After that, it got harder.

When we were both shivering and almost ready to quit, we heard an engine pulling hard up the slope toward us.

"Truck?" Penny asked.

"Sounds like it. Maybe a U-Rent."

We stared into the darkness, waiting for the truck to get close enough to see. When it reached the front of Mrs. Furrow's house, we lay down on our bellies along the ridge of the roof, our chins on our hands. The truck was going slowly by in front of the house.

"It's loaded," Penny noticed.

"Sure is," I agreed. "Is it going to turn in?"

"It's slowing down," she answered. "Let's get down to the chimney."

It was like a race. She was closer to the chimney, though, and got there first. She went up and I followed. I stood only one rung lower than she did.

But when the truck came to the driveway, it didn't turn in. Instead, whoever was driving shifted gears and went right on past the driveway, slowly speeding up again.

"Why didn't he turn in?" I asked.

"That's why," Penny pointed.

A Middleford police car cruised slowly past the front of Emma's house, going the opposite direction. The truck must have seen the police car and decided not to turn in.

"Strange," I said.

"Maybe not so strange. Makes me suspect that mean buzzard all the more," Penny whispered.

The yard light at Wickner's suddenly went out. Everything was pitch-black.

"Could he see what happened out here on the road?" Penny asked.

"I don't know. Where was he that he could see the road?"

"I don't know," Penny answered, "But—" She looked at me strangely, her eyes wide and bright in the starlight.

"But what?"

"But maybe, if he can see the road, he can also see. . .?"

"Us!" I finished her sentence. We'd been on the roof for a whole hour, watching stars, flicking the flashlight on and off, doing everything in plain sight. Suppose Wickner had been watching us watch him.

"We'd better be a little more careful," Penny said.

"I agree. Let's get down from here."

6 New Stalkings

When I got home from school on Monday, I found a message on Mom's answering machine from Mrs. Furrow: "Chad, could you and Penny come over as soon as possible?"

Her voice sounded like something was wrong. I called Penny, and we rode straight over to Mrs. Furrow's. She looked worried and she didn't even offer us cookies.

"Look what I found in my mailbox," she said, holding a sheet of paper toward us. It was a light green sheet ripped carelessly out of a spiral notebook. One corner was torn off. The note was printed in pencil, in large sloppy letters that looked like they'd been written by my little cousin:

> KEEP THOSE
> KIDS OFF YOUR ROOF
> AND OUT OF MY
> *WOODS.*

"He might be able to keep us out of his woods," Mrs. Furrow said, "but he has no right to tell me or anyone else what to do on my roof."

"What's he look like?" Penny asked.

"The same as most farmers around here—except most of them are nicer. Wickner has a mean look in his eye all the time."

"Ironman Kenyon told us to watch out for him," I said.

"And to stay out of his woods," Penny added.

"That was probably good advice," Mrs. Furrow said. "Ironman Kenyon. That would be Philip Kenyon. I think he and my son Arthur played baseball together in high school."

"He told us he went to high school with one of your sons," Penny said, nodding.

"Did Mr. Wickner grow up in this town?" I asked.

"I don't know. And from the looks of this," she shook the note, "I don't think he'll ever grow up. He has a playground brain. Always trying to get even. He likes lawsuits, too—taking people to court. I've read about several in the paper."

She was making Wickner sound more and more weird.

"But if you two see him doing anything against the law," she continued, "then you can report him to the police. When a law is being broken, it's everyone's duty to find out and to report it, note or no note."

"What makes us think he's doing something against the law?" Penny asked, as if no one had thought of the question before.

"Because he doesn't want us to catch him at it?" I asked, even though I could think of other reasons somebody might not want anyone snooping around.

We all thought about that for a minute, and then Penny said, "Because he does it at night?"

"Of course, "Mrs. Furrow said firmly. "If it were legal, he could have the trucks come and go during the day."

"I think you're right," I said. "What's that verse in the Bible about the works of darkness? It's somewhere in John. 'Men loved darkness because their deeds were evil.' And then 'Whoever does evil hates the light'? Or something like that."

"He must be able to *see* in the dark if he saw us on your roof," Penny said.

"Maybe he has a pair of those infrared binoculars," I suggested.

"He can't order us off someone else's roof, can he?" Penny asked.

"Not if we aren't doing him any harm," Mrs. Furrow said.

"Then he must be crazy," Penny suggested.

"Yes, I think he's nuts," Mrs. Furrow chuckled, and then snapped her fingers. "Speaking of nuts. I made peanut-butter cookies—just for you." She swept one of us under each of her slender arms and ushered us toward the kitchen. "I have half a notion to set up a card table on the roof and have our cookie party up there— just to spite him."

"But you're not supposed to be on the roof," Penny said.

"To get his goat, I'd go anywhere."

"If he thought we were up on the roof all the time," I said, "he'd have to quit what he's doing, wouldn't he? Or do it somewhere else?"

"Probably would," Mrs. Furrow said. "Maybe that's what's making him angry."

"We don't even know what he looks like," I said.

"I wish we could get a look at him," Penny agreed.

"About the only place I ever see him is at Petricka's Market. Usually on a Friday evening when hardly anyone else is shopping."

"Maybe we could hang out there and watch for him," I suggested.

"But we wouldn't recognize him," Penny reminded me.

"I can help," Mrs. Furrow said. "When his pickup leaves this Friday, I'll drive over and get you. We'll go to the market and watch for him."

"A stakeout," I said.

After a long pause, Penny said, "The MBI!" Mrs. Furrow and I stared at her until she explained: "The Middleford Bureau of Investigation."

"Like the FBI," I grinned.

"Well, fellow MBI members," Mrs. Furrow said, standing up and saluting, "on Friday we'll stake out Al Wickner's truck, and you can have a look at him. There's no law against that."

On Friday evening Penny and I waited for Mrs. Furrow's call in my kitchen. The MBI was eating PBC—Peanut Butter Celery.

The phone rang. "He just left," Mrs. Furrow said.

Within ten minutes, Mrs. Furrow's little Chevette pulled up in front of our house and she honked. She wouldn't have had to—Penny and I were on the porch, waiting.

We drove into Petricka's parking lot and cruised up and down a few rows, looking for the truck.

"There it is," she said excitedly, pointing. It was a green Dodge pickup, an old one, rusty and banged up. Fortunately, the gun rack in the back window was empty.

"I'm not sure we should be getting in this man's way," Mrs. Furrow said, "but as long as we're here, you two go in and look for a man wearing jeans and a wide black leather belt. He almost always wears a light-blue cotton shirt, and it's usually dirty. His hair is short and brown with gray at the temples. He's about fifty. I'd better stay in the car. He knows what I look like."

"What if we spot him?" Penny asked.

"Nothing," I said. "The MBI just investigates. In other words, we just spy."

"This is exciting," Penny whispered.

"Don't follow him out," Emma said. "You can waste a little time by buying me a couple of bags of chocolate chips." She pulled a five-dollar bill out of her purse.

We went inside the store, took a cart, and tried to act like shoppers. We went first to the baking supplies aisle and got the bags of chocolate chips so we'd really look like shoppers.

We walked slowly, sneaking peeks at the men, wondering which one was Al Wickner. There were three possibilities, all of them about the right age, all of them wearing blue jeans.

We ruled out the first one without saying a word. As we passed him in the cereal aisle, he looked at us and gave us a friendly grin. We just looked at each other and shook our heads. That man wasn't Al Wickner.

We followed one of the others for a while, but saw him buying diapers. "What does a fifty-year-old man want with diapers?" Penny whispered.

"He could be a father," I whispered back, "or a grandfather." We shook our heads. No. Not Al Wickner.

We were down to one man, but we hadn't yet gotten close enough to have a good look at him.

We pushed our cart past the checkout stands to see if he was there. He wasn't. Then we hurried up and down the aisles to see if we could catch sight of him before he left the store. As we rushed by the toothpicks and matches and napkins and were darting around a display of paper towels, Penny whispered, "Where is he?"

"Search me," I hissed back.

Just then he came around the end of the same aisle from the other direction. Our carts collided. "There he is," I blurted out.

"You two nosy brats stay out of my face," he growled at us, pulling his cart back and turning completely around. That was the last we saw of him.

We just stood there staring at each other. Finally Penny said, "He knows us."

"He does now, "I said.

We gave him plenty of time to leave the parking lot before we left the store.

We checked out, put our cart back, and walked slowly through the automatic door. Penny had two bags of chocolate chips in one hand and Mrs. Furrow's change in the other. We stepped outside, and neither of us said a word.

Penny stopped and pointed with the bags of chocolate chips. "Wickner's truck is still there," she said.

"And there's Al Wickner," I said, pointing in the other direction.

He was standing on the pavement, square in front of Mrs. Furrow's Chevette. His legs were spread, his feet planted. He shook a fist at her windshield and shouted, "You keep those kids away from me, you hear? And you keep away from me, too!"

Wickner stomped off to his pickup, got in, slammed the door, ground it into gear, and squealed out of the parking lot.

When we got to her car and crawled in, Mrs. Furrow's jaw was set and she looked angry—and stubborn. She said, "He's just an overgrown kid, that's all he is. 'Leave me alone,' he says."

"Maybe we should, Emm," Penny suggested.

"What do you say, Chad?" Mrs. Furrow asked.

"If he's up to something sinister," I said, pointing to where his truck had left the parking lot, "then Penny and I mean to find out what it is."

"Good," Mrs. Furrow said, nodding.

7 Up the Creek

"You seem to be spending a lot of time at Mrs. Furrow's," Mom said at breakfast the next morning. Saturday morning was about my best time together with Mom. She didn't work and liked to make a big breakfast—pancakes or waffles or an omelet.

"We're doing our stargazing at her house, out there where there aren't any streetlights," I said.

"It has to be more than that," Mom suggested.

I nodded. "Well—we have fun at her place."

"Doing what?"

"We eat a lot of cookies," I said, "and we're doing a kind of detective project together." I hoped she wouldn't ask too many questions.

"What sort of project?"

"We're watching one of her neighbors."

"Who?"

"Al Wickner.

"Is that the Wickner who owns Wickner's Woods?"

"That's the one."

"He sued the telephone company last year. They wanted to string a phone line underground through his property, and he wouldn't let them. I remember it from the newspaper."

"Mrs. Furrow said he liked to sue people. Mr. Kenyon doesn't like him much, either."

"Then you should listen to them and stay away from him."

I didn't say any more. Mom handed me some pancakes, and I just went on stuffing myself. When I was finishing, Penny showed up.

"Hi, Penny dear," Mom said. "Had any breakfast?"

"Mom and I had breakfast at LeCrepe," Penny said. "Just got back. I had to come over because your phone's off the hook."

"Really?" Mom said. She wiped her hands and picked up the kitchen phone. "It sure sounds dead. Check upstairs, will you, Chad?"

"Try it now," I said when I got back.

"It's okay now. What was wrong?"

"Hung up crooked," I said.

"Then it must have been off since suppertime yesterday," Mom said.

"Mr. Kenyon couldn't get through to you, so he called my house," Penny said. "He left a truck at Mrs. Furrow's early this morning."

"Wow. Well, that takes care of what we're going to do today," I said.

In twenty minutes, we were piling iron and steel into Ironman Kenyon's old truck. Mrs. Furrow wasn't home, but we knew she wouldn't mind if we got started. We hadn't been sorting long before Penny said, "We need to start a pile called 'too nice to throw away'." She was holding an old metal casting, small and brown. "This one looks like a beetle," she said, holding it up, then she tossed it beside the truck. "Let's put the stuff we like over here."

Before long I held up another casting and said, "This looks like a turtle shell." I set it beside the beetle.

"I can see why he saved some of this stuff," Penny said.

We found a metal spider hanging on the wall underneath a cloth lawnmower bag. Mr. Furrow must have welded it together out of pitchfork teeth and two big loops of chain. It really did look like a giant spider.

"That's scary," Penny said, taking it off the wall and holding it in front of her nose.

"It's dangerous, too. Each one of those legs is sharp. Eight legs? Let me see."

Penny handed me the spider. I wrapped my right hand over the body of the spider and held its sharp legs out in front of me. "It's like a shield," I said. "No one could get to me if I held this in my hand."

"That's for sure. Probably not even a dog."

"You mean like Wickner's dog."

"Of course."

"If we ever go back into those woods," I said, "I'm taking this spider with me."

By lunchtime we had a pretty good load on Mr. Kenyon's truck.

"I don't know how much more we should put on there," I said.

"Might pop the tires," Penny said, kicking one of them.

"Looks like there's enough in the garage for another load anyway, so there's no need to overload it."

"Then why don't we just go home for lunch? We can call him then."

Mrs. Furrow drove in just then and parked next to Mr. Kenyon's pickup. She got out and pointed at it. "Where did that old wreck come from?" she asked.

"It belongs to Ironman Kenyon," Penny said, then turned to me and asked, "Didn't you tell her?"

"Didn't *you*?"

"It doesn't matter, dears. It's just that when I got up this morning, that old truck was parked there. I almost called the police." She walked over to the truck and looked at all the iron and steel we'd piled into it. "That's quite a load. I'll bet you two have worked up a big hunger." We just smiled. "I haven't done my marketing yet," she went on. "I've just been down at the church meeting with the Women's Mission Society. But I can rustle you up some peanut-butter sandwiches and milk— and of course a cookie or two."

"That would be great," Penny said.

"Should I call your parents?"

"That would be great," Penny said again.

As we were standing there, Al Wickner drove out in his pickup truck. He saw us standing there together and just glared as he drove by.

"He is not a nice man," Emma said.

We followed her into the house. I wondered if we should just forget about Mr. Wickner and his mysterious truckloads of something.

66

After lunch, we just sat in silence for a while. I was leaning on my elbows on the table, nibbling at my fifth oatmeal cookie and taking sips of milk.

"I wonder what he's doing over there," Penny finally said.

"Well," Mrs. Furrow said, "if I were your age, we'd find out."

"How?" Penny asked.

"One way would be to hike up Spring Creek and have a look. That creek runs right through Wickner's Woods—and from what I remember, the creek bed is deep enough all the way through so you can hide in it." Her voice got hushed as she went on. "Too dangerous, though, with his dog and all. I don't think Al Wickner, mean as he seems, would actually hurt a kid—he'd just yell a lot. But you can't trust a mean dog."

"Maybe we could hold the dog off with the spider we found on your garage wall."

"Oh, you must mean Bill's old pitchfork spider. That might work—but I have something better."

We walked to her woodpile behind the house. I ran into the garage on the way and grabbed the spider. Leaning up against one end of her woodpile were several long sticks. She picked up one of them and wielded it like a sword, then put both hands on it and whacked it against her clothesline post.

"Feel how heavy that is," she said, handing me the stick.

I hefted it up and down, then handed it to Penny. "It *is* heavy," she said.

67

"Solid maple." Mrs. Furrow said. "I save a couple of stout straight branches like that every time I have maple cut up for firewood. I keep sticks like that all over the house. I even have one under my bed—for burglars," she laughed. "Hate the idea of hitting a dog with one, but if it's that or get bit, what are you supposed to do?"

I just shrugged.

"Mailmen carry Mace, but that has to be hard on a dog's eyes. A little whack never hurt a dog much."

"Maybe a stick would even scare a dog off," Penny said, swinging her maple stick.

"Dogs aren't *born* mean," Emma said. "I'd far rather take a stick to the man who made the dog mean in the first place. But I'll tell you this," she said intently, "if you give a dog a bit of a rap with one of my maple sticks—" She demonstrated by hitting the clothesline post again. "He won't bother you anymore."

"Makes a pretty good walking stick, too, doesn't it?" I said, taking another of the sticks and using it like a cane, then sticking it out in front of me like a sword, swish, swishing it, and using the spider for a shield. Penny picked up another of the sticks and we had a bit of a duel, until Penny came too close to whacking me on the head.

"Better quit," Mrs. Furrow said, smiling. As we puffed and got our breath back, she said, "With a stick like that, you could walk through downtown Detroit at midnight."

"Not me," Penny said.

"Wickner's Woods is scary enough," I added.

The phone rang, and Mrs. Furrow went back inside to answer it.

"Let's walk up the creek bed this afternoon," Penny said. "A creek is public property, isn't it?"

"If it isn't, it should be," I said. "We could take the spider and two of these walking sticks. We better tell Emm we're going, though, in case anything happens."

But her phone call took a long time, and we got tired of waiting.

"Let's just go," Penny said. "Nothing's going to happen anyway."

Spring Creek crossed the road about three houses beyond Mrs. Furrow's. We hid our bikes under the bridge and started walking up the creek. We each carried a maple stick, and I had the spider in my other hand. We whispered as we walked, and we were glad we'd worn our metal-loading clothes and shoes. We had to wade in the creek several times because the brush along the bank was so thick.

A couple of times we climbed up the bank and peeked over. I was sure we were on Wickner's property, but as we got farther and farther up the creek, our peeks over the bank showed that we were almost out of the woods. Finally we saw a small field, completely surrounded by woods. Ahead of us, near the creek, lay a large pile of dirt. Had someone dumped the dirt there, I wondered, or was someone digging a hole?

We didn't dare go any farther in daylight. "Let's come back at night," I said.

Penny looked at me, and I knew we were both thinking the same thing—it would be awfully scary walking up that creek bed at night. Dangerous, too, with that dog around somewhere. But how else would we find out what was going on?

She shrugged. "I don't know. Maybe. It would have to be some night when the truck comes."

"You think he's digging a hole out in that field?"

"You mean by the dirt pile? Could be. Maybe he's burying something."

"Maybe the bodies of the snoopy kids he murders," I whispered.

We both shuddered. As we started back down the creek bed, the wind must have changed, because I smelled a funny smell I hadn't smelled before. A hardware-store smell.

When we'd gone about halfway back to the road, Penny pointed to something else we'd missed on the way in, on the opposite bank of the creek. "Look at that," she said. There were five or six dead fish washed up into the branches of a bush. We walked farther downstream and saw several more dead fish.

What was that smell? And why were there so many dead fish?

I poked one of the dead fish with my maple stick. "Well," I said, "maybe this will turn out to be Earthkeepers business after all."

Marked Truck and Dirty Stalkings

8

"Wow—look at us," Penny said as we pushed our bikes out from under the bridge and up onto the road.

We were covered with mud up to our knees, and our clothes had burrs all over them. We picked burrs off each other, cleaned ourselves off as well as we could, and then rode toward home.

"We didn't learn much, did we?" Penny finally said as we pedaled along.

"Not a whole lot. At least we learned we could hike up the creek and watch that field. And we learned that whatever suspicious thing is going on at Wickner's place is hurting the creek and killing the fish—and making some kind of weird smell."

"And all of that has to be related somehow to whatever that truck is bringing in there at night," Penny said.

"Wish we could mark the truck somehow and then go down and snoop in it the next day. That'd tell us something."

"Couldn't we run out from behind Emm's tree and just mark the truck as it turned onto the road?" she asked.

"I think so," I said. "What would we mark it with? Spray paint?"

"No. U-Rent might get mad at us for that. How about one of our Earthkeepers bumper stickers?"

"Good idea."

When I got home, Mom told me Emma Furrow had called. "Weren't you just out there?" she asked.

I nodded, and then explained, "We stopped to play around in Spring Creek on the way home." I pointed at my dirty pantlegs, and my mom rolled her eyes.

Emma asked where we'd gone off to without saying good-bye, and then invited us out for the evening. She suggested that we not ride our bikes but walk out, sometime after 8:00, and that she'd drive us home a little after 10:00. "I've been listening for those trucks," she said, "now that you've called my attention to them. There have been several, and they always come between 9:00 and 10:00. I can usually hear Wickner's tractor running, too. It runs a long time after the truck leaves."

"We'll be there," I said. I hung up and headed for the shower.

Penny and I arrived at Mrs. Furrow's just at dusk. She had made an apple pie. We ate, talked, and then went up on the roof to watch the stars for a while. Nothing was happening at Wickner's, so we came back in the house about 9:30. Ten minutes later, the U-Rent truck showed up.

Mrs. Furrow snapped off the lights, and we ran to the front window to watch. There was no one around this time to frighten the driver away, so he turned right into Wickner's driveway.

"What do we do now?" Emma asked.

"We ought to try to mark the truck," I said. I pulled the Earthkeepers bumper sticker out of my back pocket and held it up.

"How are you going to do that?" Mrs. Furrow asked.

"I'll just run out from behind your tree," I said, "when he's coming out of Wickner's driveway. I'll get behind the truck and just slap the bumper sticker on the door."

"Who said *you* were going to do it?" Penny said. "It was my idea."

"Only the bumper sticker part," I said. "It was my idea to mark the truck."

"Okay," she agreed finally, "but only if I get to do the next exciting thing, whatever it is."

"While you're doing that," Emma said, "I'll turn my car around. Penny and I will be sitting in it and ready to go. All you have to do is run behind the truck, mark it, then run back here and jump into the car with us. The three of us will follow him."

It almost worked. Almost. Trouble was, the driver must have spotted me in his rear-view mirror. I got the Earthkeepers sticker on the back door of the truck all right, but then he slammed on his brakes and stopped the truck, so instead of heading back toward Emma's car, I kept right on running. I ran across the road, into the ditch, and back toward the creek. I took a quick look over my shoulder, and when I didn't see anyone running after me, I ducked behind a bush and waited.

A minute or two later I heard the truck door slam, and then the truck drove away. I ran back to Emma and Penny in the car. We took off after the truck.

"We saw the whole thing," Penny said as Mrs. Furrow drove. "The driver got out right in front of Mrs. Furrow's driveway—but it's so dark out here with no streetlights that I don't think he saw you running down the ditch, and he didn't even look over where we were sitting in the car. He shook his fist at you and then looked at the back of the truck. But he didn't act like he noticed the bumper sticker."

The truck was out of sight before we ever left the driveway, and we drove all over town looking for it but never found it. Finally, at about 10:30, Mrs. Furrow took Penny and me home.

Before we said good-bye, Penny and I decided to meet after school on Monday to ride our bikes down to the U-Rent lot.

As it turned out, Penny and I were together before that.

In the principal's office.

It came as a big surprise. We were called out of class in the middle of the afternoon and told to go directly to the office. My first thought was, *Did something happen to Mom?* Why else would I get called to the office? But then why would they have called Penny, too?

The principal wasn't in his office; he was pacing around in the secretary's space looking grumpy. "Someone in my office wants to talk to you," he said. "He asked that it be done in private."

Penny and I gave each other a puzzled look and went slowly into the principal's office. A man was looking out of the window with his back to us. Then he turned around—it was Officer Monty Irwin, from the Middleford Police Department.

"Hi," he said with a big smile.

The smile made it easier. At least I knew nothing terrible was wrong.

"I'm sorry to have to do this, kids," he finally said.

"Do what?" I asked.

"I have a complaint lodged against you two."

"For *what?*" we both said together, shocked.

"Do you know about Minnesota's new stalking law?"

"Not really," Penny said. I shook my head.

"I'm not sure it really applies in this case, and I'm not sure he could make it stick in court, but Al Wickner has lodged a complaint against you two and your friend Emma Furrow for following him around and harassing him."

Penny's eyes went wide. Mine probably did, too.

"We've been watching his place," I admitted. "We didn't think it was against the law or anything."

"He seems to think it is," Mr. Irwin said. "I agreed to come over here and talk to you because I know you kids and because, frankly, I didn't think this was important enough to get your parents all worked up over—although I'll probably have to tell them about it, too, at some point.

"We've had our share of trouble with Wickner, to tell you the truth," Mr. Irwin went on. "He's always calling us about something or suing someone. But it's our job to follow up on these things—so here I am. He probably doesn't have much of a case, but he does have a right to his privacy. I think you two should just stay out of his hair."

"I guess," I said.

"Have you talked to Mrs. Furrow?" Penny asked.

"I called her on the phone. She was pretty upset about Wickner's calling us, but she did admit that the three of you were playing a kind of spying game. She mentioned the MBI. What's that?"

There was a long silence, then Penny said, "I made that up. It means the Middleford Bureau of Investigation."

Mr. Irwin exploded into a long, loud laugh. Through the frosted glass on the door I could see the principal looking in to see what was so funny.

"Well, you two had better leave the investigating to us," Mr. Irwin chuckled when he was done laughing. "You seem to have gotten into more than your share of danger—in the last year anyway."

"I guess so," I said. "But people do mysterious things. We can't help but notice."

"If Mr. Wickner or anyone else does anything wrong, you just call *us*. We'll take care of it."

"Thanks," Penny said.

"That's all for now, kids. If you stay away from him, this matter won't go any further."

"That's fine with us," I said.

"Good. We're agreed then."

He shook hands with both of us, asked some questions about Earthkeepers, and then we were sent back to class with hallway passes.

After school we met as planned. "Let's still go down to U-Rent and see if we can find our Earthkeepers sticker on one of their trucks. I don't see how Mr. Wickner can complain about that."

"Right," Penny said, swinging her foot over the bar of her mountain bike. "Beat you there."

She did, but not by much. We were puffing hard as we locked our bikes together against a street sign and walked into the lot. We passed the trailers and headed straight for the big utility vans. "There it is," Penny said, when she saw our bumper sticker on a truck.

"Let's ask if we can look inside it," I said.

We went into the rental building and saw the same man we had talked to before. "You two going to rent a trailer after all?" he asked, recognizing us.

I didn't want to lie to him. I just said, "We already started to haul our metal, but I thought we should look at a rental truck, just in case."

"What size truck you think you need?"

"We'd like to look inside of one, just to see how big it is," Penny said.

"Yeah," I added. "Maybe one like that third one out there." I pointed.

"It's not locked. All you have to do is pull that lever up like this," he demonstrated with his hand, "then roll the door up into the ceiling."

"Thanks," I said.

We walked out into the lot again. Penny lifted the lever the way he had shown us, and then pushed the rear door up. It worked just like my grandma's rolltop desk. "Nothing to it," Penny said.

When the van door opened, I smelled the same smell I had smelled along the creek.

"Funny smell in here," Penny said. "Hey—I smelled that same smell out along the creek at Wickner's."

So she had smelled it out there, too. Neither of us had mentioned it to the other. Bad detective work.

"Look at the rings on the floor." There were five of them. Big rings. As big as if you drew around the outside of a garbage can cover with a brown felt pen.

Penny bent over and ran her finger around one of the rings, then put it to her nose. "The smell is coming from the rings," she said.

9 Spider Man

We rode over to my garage from the U-Rent lot and talked for a long time about what Officer Irwin had said. We weren't even sure we should go back to Mrs. Furrow's house again.

"But he can't keep us from visiting her," Penny frowned. "Can he? That's un-American."

"That's right. This is a free country. Let's at least go out and talk to her."

We hopped on our bikes and started out.

"Maybe this whole Wickner's Woods deal is stupid," Penny said as we rode. "Maybe there's really nothing going on, and we've been fooling ourselves."

"But if that's true," I said, pulling up alongside the curb so we could talk for a minute, "there are a lot of things that don't make any sense."

"You mean the smell?"

"Yeah, that," I said, "and the rings on the floor of the truck."

"And what about that pile of dirt?" Penny added. "And the fish?"

"All that stuff fits together somehow," I said. "We just haven't figured out how yet."

"It's easier doing Earthkeeper stuff."

"I'll bet this *is* Earthkeeper stuff. Something weird is happening to that creek. Besides, this whole thing started when we were hauling metal, remember? Those whole woods are full of it."

"We've been so busy with the MBI," Penny said, "that we never called Mr. Kenyon to tell him his truck was full."

"We can call him from Mrs. Furrow's."

We rode on in silence. When we got to Mrs. Furrow's driveway, Penny pointed and said, "Look!"

I didn't see at first what she was pointing at. The truck was in the driveway, and everything seemed the same—until I took another look at the truck. It was a different color, and when we rode up to it, I saw it was empty. "He brought us a different truck," I said. "Now we have a perfectly good excuse for being here."

"Right."

Emma Furrow came out the back door just then and noticed us standing by the truck. "I called Mr. Kenyon," she said. "Ironman? Is that what you call him?" We nodded. She went on. "I told him his truck was full, and he offered to bring another one. We had coffee and a nice chat about the old days when he and my Brian were in high school. He's such a nice man." But her smile disappeared almost immediately. "Some people aren't so nice," she said, and pulled an envelope out of her side pocket. She shook it toward Wickner's Woods. "Stalking and harassment, is it?" she shouted across the road.

"He's taking me to court, that rascal." She shook the envelope toward his place again. "I got a subpoena," she said. "I have to go to court."

"We *have* been pestering him," Penny admitted.

"But that's because he's up to something," I reminded them.

"Well, I wish we could prove it before they call me in," Mrs. Furrow said. "Otherwise, I may be in big trouble."

We all stood there quietly, looking at each other. None of us seemed willing to say what I'm sure we were all thinking. After all, Penny and I had been warned by Officer Irwin, and now Mrs. Furrow was in trouble, too. But maybe she'd be in even bigger trouble if we didn't do something. Finally I decided to say it. "Should we give it one more try?"

Mrs. Furrow looked thoughtful. "Well, we'll have to be more careful," she said.

"And we'd better really find something this time," I warned. "Otherwise—" I didn't need to say it. We all knew.

"We might just as well load metal until dark," Penny said.

By supper time we had almost emptied the garage. There were a few things still hanging on the wall—a coil of rope and a few garden tools. Mrs. Furrow had told us a long story one day about how her husband, Bill, had used that rope to teach her to tie fancy knots. She had even tried to show us how to tie some of them, but it had seemed pretty complicated.

Penny and I had made a pile of metal things we weren't sure about—some old hand tools and a lawn fertilizer that didn't look like it worked anymore. We called Mrs. Furrow out to help us decide.

"Take it all," she said. "Who knows—" She pulled out the subpoena again and waved it toward us. "Maybe by this time next year I'll be in jail." She put the envelope away with a shake of her head. "A clean garage," she said. "I can't believe it. You kids have done me a wonderful service. You get cookies and milk for the rest of your lives."

"If you're not in jail," Penny whispered. Emma smiled and gave her a hug.

As we were getting ready to ride our bikes home, Emma asked, "Do you want to come back tonight?"

"We could work on our star map," Penny said.

"We could maybe watch the road a bit, too," I said.

At 8:45 Penny and I were in Emma Furrow's back yard, lying flat on our backs, looking at the first stars. We decided, just in case Wickner had infrared binoculars— or could see in the dark—that we'd better stay off the roof. Mrs. Furrow offered to watch for the truck from inside the house.

Before long Mrs. Furrow came to the back door and waved us in. We rushed into the living room. "It came," she said. "Drove up his driveway just now. There's no use fooling with the truck. It's already in there—and when it comes out it's empty."

"I wish we could see what's in it," Penny said.

"Whatever comes on that truck is heavy—and they unload it. He has to do *something* with it."

"That's why he uses his tractor," I suggested.

84

"And that," Emma Furrow said, "is why I usually hear the tractor running for a long time after the truck has gone." Emma slapped her thigh and said, "I don't care what the doctor told me, I'm going up on the roof to watch."

The ladder was still against the back of the roof. Mrs. Furrow climbed up and disappeared.

"Should we go up there with her?" Penny asked. "Or better yet—should we go back up the creek and see what they're doing back there?"

"At night?" I couldn't believe it—with that dog and everything.

"We could do it. We've already been there once. There's no deep water. Nothing dangerous."

Except a man-eating dog. Besides—"Emma would never let us, not after what Mr. Irwin said and everything," I said.

"She doesn't need to know. She's on the roof. We can leave right now. Wickner wouldn't dare do anything to us," Penny whispered, "not now. He's named our names. If something should happen to any one of us on or near his place, he'd be the first person they'd suspect."

I didn't want to go back there. And Penny must have sensed that I didn't, because she used her most powerful argument: "Do you want Emm to go to jail?" she asked.

"No, I don't," I said, "but what about Wickner's dog? You can't blame a farm dog for biting trespassers." Penny just stood there and looked at me. I didn't want her to think I was a chicken, and I didn't want Emma to go to jail, and I didn't want Wickner to get by with any-

85

thing. "If we take sticks," I finally said, "and the spider—maybe we'll be okay."

"Let's go for it." She held up her thumbs. We hadn't done that for a while. We pulled earlobes and pressed thumbprints.

"I'll get the sticks," she said. "You get the spider and Emm's big flashlight from the garage."

We were running toward the creek when we heard Emma shout our names from the roof. We heard the truck coming back out of Wickner's lane at almost exactly the same time. We just made it over the edge of the creek bank when the truck lights swept across above us. We sat still for a minute or two and listened to the truck rumbling away down the road, growing fainter. Then we started up the creek.

After about ten minutes, we'd made it far enough up the creek that we were starting to get really nervous. We could hear the tractor moving around up in the field.

We climbed up the bank and took a look. The tractor was moving toward the big hole with its loader bucket held high off the ground, but we couldn't see what was in it. Mr. Wickner, or whoever was driving it, was working with only one dim light on the tractor.

"We have to get closer," I whispered.

"I know," Penny whispered back. "But this is scary."

"It's for Emma." I probably didn't need to remind her.

We slid back down the bank and went further upstream. We found a good place to climb up and had just started working our way up through the brush when suddenly we both froze. From the top of the bank came a deep snarling growl. Wickner's dog. He was waiting for us.

I wanted to run, but I knew he'd just chase us, and he could run a lot faster than we could. "Get the flashlight ready," I whispered close to Penny's ear, my voice shaking. I slid the spider onto the end of my maple walking stick and pushed it up in front of us. When the spider was up over the edge of the bank and kind of hanging in midair like a giant phantom insect, I whispered, "Now!"

Penny aimed the flashlight toward the spider and then flipped it on. Her aim was good—the beam hit the spider right on, first thing. I had tried to get the spider as close to where the dog's growls seemed to be coming from as I could, so he wouldn't miss it, and I guess I was close enough, because the next thing we heard was him *yip-yip-yipping* across the field. The sound softly disappeared.

"He's afraid of spiders," Penny snorted, and slugged my shoulder. I pulled the spider back down.

We crawled up the bank then and watched.

Mr. Wickner, if he was the one driving the tractor, seemed to be driving down into the big trench and unloading whatever was in the bucket of his tractor, then going back to the farm buildings to get more.

"When he goes back this time," I said, "I'm going to run over to that hole and see what's in it."

"I'll go with you," Penny said.

I shook my head. "We shouldn't both go. One of us should stay here with the flashlight to warn the other when Wickner comes back."

87

She opened her mouth to argue, and then realized that there wasn't time. "Okay," she mumbled, and I hopped partway over the bank to get ready.

The minute the tractor seemed far enough away, I ran for the pile of dirt. There was no moon, only starlight—barely enough light to see by.

When I got to the trench, I could see where the tractor had been driving in on a sloped runway. I ran around to that end of the hole and ran down the runway into the trench. The hole was deeper than I was tall—and it was even darker in there than it had been up a ground level. I moved ahead carefully, with my arms out in front of me—until I banged my knee into something big, cold, and round, something that went *bong* when I hit it.

I rubbed my knee first, and then I felt the thing with my hand. Big. Hard—metal, it felt like. Round, like a giant tin can.

And suddenly it all fell into place. I knew exactly what Wickner was up to. All of our hunches had been right. And all I had to do was get out of that hole and tell the right people.

Then I heard the tractor. I'd been so busy thinking that I hadn't heard it coming back. It was close. I turned and ran a few steps back up the runway, but it was no use; I stopped. The tractor's dim light was coming right toward me like a snorting one-eyed monster. Why hadn't Penny shined the light and warned me? Maybe she had. How would I have seen it down here in the hole?

I backed down in the hole again. The bucket of the tractor was loaded and aimed right at me. I was

about to be crushed between what was already in the trench and what was loaded in the bucket of the tractor. The tractor was almost to the runway—I'd never make it out that way. Maybe I could scramble up the steeper sides of the hole—but then he'd see me.

Well, I had no choice. I was just about to jump for it when I saw flashes of light hitting the side of the tractor. I scrambled a little way up the side of the pit to watch, and saw the driver's face, lit by flashes of light from the direction of the creek. It was Mr. Wickner, all right. And the light must have been Penny trying to distract him.

With a snort, the tractor turned in her direction and chugged toward the creek. This was my chance, and I didn't waste any time. I scrambled up out of the hole and ran toward the creek bed farther upstream. When I got there, in spite of the darkness, I dived over the bank, rolled over once, and came up running. I tripped when I hit the water and fell on my hands and knees. Now I was soaked.

I wanted to go back downstream toward Penny, but that's right where Mr. Wickner was. I decided my best chance was to crawl up the other bank and put some distance between Wickner and me. I scrambled up the bank and ran through the trees, glancing back over my shoulder every second or two.

Oof! I smashed into something big and sprawled across it, sliding clear across and falling into the grass on the other side. I jumped back up to my feet and looked back to see what I'd hit. I strained my eyes in the darkness—a car. I had run into a car. It was too dark to see it well, but I felt it—the paint was smooth, no rust. It wasn't some hunk of junk left out in the woods to rust away. What was a car doing here on the far bank of Spring Creek in Wickner's Woods? Was this his getaway car?

I hadn't heard anything from Penny, so I crept back to the bank of the creek and watched as Wickner stopped the tractor at the lip of the creek bed, right where Penny had shined the light. He slid off the tractor seat and walked to the edge, peering over the bank.

I said a quick prayer for Penny. I guess it was answered, because Wickner soon gave up, backed up the tractor, and rumbled off toward the trench.

I crawled back down into the creek bed and made my scratchy, wet, and shin-bumping way back through and along the water in almost complete darkness, wondering where Penny was and hoping she was okay. At least I knew Wickner hadn't gotten her.

I couldn't wait to tell Penny and Mrs. Furrow what Wickner was up to. If I was right, Wickner wouldn't dare take Emma to court. If I was right, this was another Earthkeepers mystery after all!

10

A Jar
of Water

"Chad? Is that you?"

Penny must have heard me rattling and splashing down in the creek bed. I didn't see any reason to be quiet now that I was so close to the road. Penny's voice came from high on the bank, under the bridge.

"It's me. Are you okay?" I asked.

"I'm fine," she whisper-spoke. "How about you?"

I could still feel the bumps and bruises from crashing over that car out in the woods. "Nothing broken. Let's get over to Emm's."

When we got into Mrs. Furrow's back yard, she was climbing down the ladder. She sounded a little put out with us. "I've been up on the roof, then back down here ready to call 911, then back on the roof—you went over there, didn't you?"

We both nodded.

"What happened? Are you all right? Just *look* at you, Chad," Mrs. Furrow said, "for heaven's sake. You're soaked. You look like you've been in a hurricane. Are you all right?"

"I've scratched and skinned myself all over," I said, "and banged the same knee twice. I'm okay, though." I laughed. "I think I'm still too scared to be cold." Penny didn't look much better than I did. Her feet were wet and her face was smudged.

"Well, come in and let's clean you both up and look you over."

"I need to do one more thing before I clean up," I said. "Could I have a glass jar with a lid—like a mayonnaise jar or something?"

Emma looked at me strangely, but she said, "Sure—I have lots of those." She slipped in through the kitchen door.

"What's up, Chad?" Penny asked while she was inside.

"I want a water sample," I said.

"From where?"

"The creek."

Emma came back out and handed me the jar. "Come on," I said to Penny, "and bring the flashlight. We'll be right back," I said to Mrs. Furrow.

"Phooey on that," Mrs. Furrow said. "I'm coming, too."

"I hope I can get this flashlight switch to work," Penny mumbled.

"I could have told you about that switch, if you had asked," Emma said as we walked toward the creek through Hensley's backyard.

"If we had asked," Penny grinned, still fumbling with the switch, "you wouldn't have let us go."

"Here," Emma said, reaching for the flashlight. "Let me show you how I do it."

So now I knew why Penny hadn't warned me sooner with the flashlight. The switch didn't always work.

We went back to the bridge. I waded into the middle of the creek—I was already soaked anyway, so I figured it didn't matter—and scooped the jar full of water. Penny shined the flashlight for me.

"Why are you doing that, Chad?" she asked.

"If I'm right," I said, holding up the jar as I screwed on the lid, "this jar of water is going to prove Wickner is a pretty serious bad guy. It won't be Wickner's Woods anymore—it'll be Jailbird's Woods."

"What did he do?" Penny asked.

"Let's not stand here in someone else's backyard," Mrs. Furrow half-whispered. "Come back to my place. You can tell us there."

Penny and I took off our wet tennis shoes at the back door and dragged ourselves into the kitchen.

"You two look like refugees from a typhoon. And you're right—if you had asked, I never would have let you go. Now your parents won't let you come over here anymore."

"It wasn't your fault," Penny said softly.

"All I could do was keep going up on the roof to watch," Emma said. "I was praying for you the whole time."

"We should have been praying for you," Penny smiled. "The doctor told you to stay off the roof."

"This was an emergency," she said firmly.

I set the jar of water on the kitchen table. Penny and Emma stared at it. Penny finally spoke. "Okay, Chad. Now. Tell us what the water means."

"When I was down in that trench in Wickner's field, I ran into something big and round and metal that went *bong*. It was dark, but I felt around. I think what I was feeling were several metal barrels. Just suppose Wickner is burying something he shouldn't be, something poisonous, out in his field. And just suppose whatever he's burying is getting into the creek —"

"Wow!" Penny shouted. "Can we prove it?"

I held up the jar of water. "Someone can," I said.

"Maybe that's what's killing the fish!" Penny said.

"Toxic waste," Emma Furrow said. "There's big money in illegal toxic waste. It's very expensive to haul it to legal disposal sites, so some dishonest businesses pay people to dispose of it illegally, where it can get into the water. I'll bet that's what Al Wickner is up to."

"Who do we tell?" I asked.

"The EPA," Mrs. Furrow said firmly. "The Environmental Protection Agency."

"How do we find them?" Penny asked.

"We can look in the St. Paul directory," she said, pulling out a thick white pages from under her telephone stand.

"Should we call the police?" I asked.

"You bet we should," Mrs. Furrow said, turning suddenly and shaking a fist toward Wickner's Woods. "If he's really polluting our creek, the sooner we stop him the better. By the way, did he see either of you?"

"No," I said. "I'm almost sure he didn't. But he saw the flashlight, so he knew there was *somebody* back there tonight."

"And all his dog saw was the spider," Penny laughed. Then I laughed.

"Where is the spider," I asked Penny.

"It must still be there," Penny shrugged. Then after a pause, "What if he finds it?"

"It won't mean a thing to him," I said, "but it means a lot to me. I want it back."

When we explained about the dog and the spider to Mrs. Furrow, she laughed harder than both of us, then dialed the number of the police station and asked for Monty Irwin. I suggested he come in a plain car, park it back behind the garage, and use the back door. "Sounds mysterious," he chuckled. "Is this another MBI caper?"

"Same one," I said.

Ten minutes later Officer Irwin sat in Mrs. Furrow's kitchen drinking coffee and eating rhubarb pie. We told him the whole story.

"That's a serious accusation," he said. "If you're right, he's in big trouble. If you're wrong, though, *you're* in trouble. He's already charged you with harassment. And I told you to stay away from him."

"But why else would he be burying steel barrels in his field after dark?" Mrs. Furrow asked.

"I don't know. But remember—there may be a good explanation. Our dispatcher takes calls every day about suspicious-looking activity. Most of them turn out to be nothing."

"But if there's something in the water ..." I said.

"Yes," Monty agreed, picking up the jar and peering through it, "yes, if there's something in the water, then we have reason to investigate. Do you mind if I take this?"

"I have dozens of those jars," Emma said,

"And there's a whole creek full of the same water," Penny added.

"I guess it's not the kind of evidence you guard with your life," Monty laughed. "I'll take it to St. Paul tomorrow. The EPA has labs. They can check. Meanwhile, *don't* go back over there. Leave him alone until we have some evidence." He looked at each of us sternly, one at a time. "It's my job to protect that man's privacy. If there's an investigation to be carried out, it'll be carried out by people who are authorized to do it."

The next afternoon, a hall monitor came to my last class and handed me a note: "You are to call Mrs. Furrow," it said, "555–6017."

I found Penny the minute school was out. She had the same note. "Let's go to my place," I said. "We can call from there."

With Penny on the kitchen phone and me on the upstairs extension, we called Mrs. Furrow. "Did they learn something already?" Penny asked.

"I guess they don't fool around at that lab," Emma said. "They found traces of several toxic things in that water, things that don't show up in farm creeks. Let me see. I wrote them down on my pad here: formaldehyde, toluene, and xylene."

"What are they?" Penny asked.

"The EPA lab thinks they might be solvents from paint shops or auto body shops."

"That's it then!" I crowed. "We've got him!"

"I think so," Mrs. Furrow agreed. "I offered to let the police watch from my house, but I made them promise to let the three of us watch with them."

"Great," I said.

"Good for you," Penny added.

"Well, you two got us into this," she said. "If we find out he's polluting the water around here, this whole town will have you two to thank." Then she paused, and said in a more serious tone, "I don't think you two should ride your bikes out here anymore. Now that we know there's actually a crime being committed, I don't think you two should be riding around these streets alone, especially at night. When you want to come out, you just telephone and I'll come and get you."

"That's a lot of bother for you," I said.

"Bother? I haven't had so much fun in years! Let's start tonight. Mr. Irwin plans to be here every night from 7:00 to 11:00. Supposing I come and get you around 7:15. He can watch while I'm getting you."

There's no way they can show on TV how boring stakeouts can be. We watched for the whole evening. Monty Irwin sat in the front room facing the front windows. He spent most of the time reading a folder of police reports. A cup of coffee and a plate of cookies sat on the coffee table in front of him.

From time to time, Emma Furrow walked in with her old coffee pot and filled his cup. "That's the best coffee I've had in years," he said, closing his eyes and smelling the steam from his cup.

"You want good coffee," she replied, "get rid of your automatic coffee maker." He just laughed.

No one came to Wickner's.

On the drive home, I said, "I think Wickner has a car parked on the other side of the woods. Maybe it's a getaway car. Is there a road going out the other side of the woods?"

"You know, I think there is," Mrs. Furrow said slowly. "Back before Wickner leased that place, Bill and I used to—"

"Did you say 'lease'?" I interrupted. "You mean he doesn't own his own farm?"

"That's right," Mrs. Furrow said. "But that's not unusual. Farmland is expensive, and many farmers don't have the kind of down payment or credit they'd need to buy a farm. So they lease. Old Wickner's been leasing that land for—my word—must be forty years now. Anyway, before that, Bill and I used to hike those woods. We used to know every inch of them. Yes, there *is* a road. It comes out on the northwest corner."

"Then that *could* be a getaway car," Penny insisted. "If he's made a lot of money burying illegal toxic waste, and if he thinks—" she grinned— "if he thinks the Earthkeepers are hot on his trail—"

"Sure," I said. "He'll just disappear with the money and let someone else clean up his mess. What does he have to lose? He doesn't even own the farm."

"It would all be cash, too," Emma said. "No one writes a check to pay for something illegal. Well, I'll call Monty Irwin about the car when I get home," Emma said.

When we got near Penny's house I asked to be dropped off. "I'll walk from here," I said.

After Emma drove away, I said to Penny, "What if tomorrow after school we ride our bikes along the road on the north side of the woods? Maybe we could find that road."

Penny looked skeptical. "You know what Monty Irwin would say about that," she said.

"I know, but Monty Irwin doesn't know about the getaway car yet. This way, we can get the license number. Besides, that car is only about a little way from our spider. We could get the spider back, have a quick look at the car, and get out in less than ten minutes."

I should have known things never go quite like I planned.

I'm up for it," Penny said

"Don't you dare," was all Emma Furrow said.

A Tree Trunk and a Car Trunk

Right after school the next day, we rode around to the north side of Wickner's Woods on our bikes. The road that went back into the woods to his getaway car was just a path, really, and so overgrown with weeds and brush that we had to ride back and forth a couple of times before we found it. It didn't look like anybody had driven on it all summer long.

"Are you sure it wasn't just some old junker car that's been sitting there for years?" Penny asked.

"It was shiny," I said. "Or smooth, at least. It wasn't rusty."

"Okay. So—what do we do now?"

"Well," I said, "we could go in and get our spider back."

We looked at each other, neither of us too sure. Then we both decided at the same time, without saying anything. We hid our bikes in some bushes and began walking in along the road, each of us walking down one of the two dirt tracks on the weedy road that wound through the trees. Wickner's Woods was old, with lots of fallen trees—and a few dead ones that looked like they were ready to fall.

"Look at this tree," I said. I pushed against it, reaching as high as I could on its trunk. The tree wiggled dangerously.

"Watch out," Penny warned.

"You know," I said, "I think if we threw Mr. Furrow's rope over that branch up there, the two of us could pull this tree right over."

"Probably. But why?" Penny asked.

"If we pulled it over in this direction," I said, letting my arm show how the tree could fall.

"Yes!" Penny said. "Across the road! He could never get over that tree with a car."

"Should we get the rope and do it right now?"

Penny shook her head. "He might see it today and move it."

I nodded. "So we should pull the tree over just when he's getting ready to leave, right?"

"I think so. And then call the police."

Suddenly a dog barked, probably Wickner's. "Let's get out of here," Penny said.

"Right," I said. "The spider can wait."

Back at home, we could hardly wait for dark and for Emma to come for us. When we got to her house, Mr. Irwin was already there. "Maybe we'll get lucky tonight, kids," he said as we walked in. He was sitting in the dim light of the living room, watching out the front window.

"I hope so," Emma said from the dining room.

"Although, to tell the truth," he said, "I guess I'd be glad to find out this was all a mistake. But you can't argue with what was in that jar of water."

"Why don't you just go in and arrest him?" Penny asked.

"We could. But we also want to catch whoever is driving that truck. There are businesses behind this, businesses that are breaking the law to save money. They're paying Wickner and that driver to dispose of barrels illegally. We want to get them all if we can."

"They ought to register every single barrel," Emma said indignantly.

"Actually, they do," Mr. Irwin said. "I was talking to the EPA about it. Every barrel being shipped today has a serial number stamped into it. They're easier to trace than counterfeit money."

"Then you should be able to tell whose barrels they are and arrest them," Penny said.

"Trouble is," Mr. Irwin said, "there are still too many unregistered barrels around—old barrels. The crooks use them. They're impossible to trace."

"You want to catch them in the act, then, do you?" Emma asked.

"We sure do. I have two police cars on alert—and we can call a traffic helicopter to light up the area if we want to."

"Sounds like all that truck has to do now is show up," Emma said.

"And that," Penny said, "is just what it's doing." She pointed out the front window. There, coming up the road, was a U-rent truck, sagging low on its springs—heavily loaded.

"Dial 911 for me," Monty Irwin said to Mrs. Furrow. "They're waiting for my call. We're all ready for this."

Behind me I could hear Emma dialing, then saying, "Hold on, please. Officer Irwin has a message for you."

She handed Mr. Irwin the phone. He watched until the truck had turned in at Wickner's drive, then ordered, "Send out the two cars right away. Tell them that I want one on each end of the road to pick up the U-Rent truck. Put me on line five with the dispatcher now."

Everything moved fast after that. Within ten minutes, the dispatcher reported that the two police cars were posted on the road at either end of Wickner's Woods. "When the truck comes back out," Mr. Irwin explained, one of the two cars will stop it. Then the other one will come here and pick me up and we'll go have a little talk with Mr. Wickner. I have the search warrant right here in my pocket," he said to Emma, patting his heart.

Everything went just as he'd planned it. The truck pulled back out onto the road and disappeared, and a few minutes later the dispatcher reported over the phone that the driver had been arrested.

When the police car pulled into Mrs. Furrow's driveway, Officer Irwin stood and said, "I have to go—but I need someone to stay by this telephone."

"Glad to," Mrs. Furrow said, taking the phone from him and putting it to her ear. "Is that you, Cindy?" she said to the dispatcher. "This is Emma Furrow." She listened a minute and then said, "Oh, I'm fine, dear. And how's your new baby?"

"Police business, remember?" Monty smiled as he headed toward the back door.

Emma was saying, "Sorry," as Monty Irwin disappeared out the door.

"Are we just supposed to sit here?" Penny groaned.

"You could pray that no one gets hurt," Mrs. Furrow reminded us.

"In that case, we'd better pray that no one runs into Wickner's dog," Penny smiled.

"They should have our spider," I said.

"We should have told them were it was," Penny grinned. "You did tell them about the getaway car, didn't you?" she asked Emma.

"Oh no!" Emma gasped. "No, not you Cindy," she said into the phone. Then with a hand over the mouthpiece, she said to us, "Everything was so hectic I completely forgot. Did either of you tell anyone?"

We shook our heads.

"Oh, Cindy, you won't believe what I forgot," Mrs. Furrow said, turning her attention back to the phone, her expensive tennis shoes tapping rapidly against the floor in frustration.

"We've got to get over there," Penny whispered to me.

Penny grabbed the flashlight from the kitchen table on our way out. "Get the rope from the garage," she hissed as we rushed into the back yard.

"The tree," I whispered.

I had the rope, and Penny had the flashlight. We ran down the road and across the bridge. On the other side of the bridge, we went down through the ditch, up the other side, and across another section of Wickner's rickety fence. There was no reason to walk in the creek bed this time. Wickner would be busy with the police over near his buildings—or else he'd be out in his field, burying the barrels. He'd never notice us or our flashlight.

We ran as fast as we could through the woods, ducking branches, stepping over fallen logs, and following the creek. Before long we saw something reflect the flashlight ahead of us. "There it is," I said, as we walked into the small clearing with the car in it. It was a gray, normal-looking sedan, several years old. A perfect getaway car, because it was the kind of car no one would notice.

"We could let the air out of his tires," Penny whispered, panting for breath.

I shook my head. "I don't want to stay around the car that long. If he's going to use it, he'll be here any minute. All he has to do when the police come to arrest him is say he wants to get his hat or his wallet, go back into the house, and disappear out the back door. They'll never find him."

"Then let's follow the road to that tree and pull it down."

It took a few minutes to find the tree in the dark. When we did, Penny shined the light up into the branches. On the third try I was able to throw the rope over one of them. We wrapped the rope around the tree, I made some sort of slipknot, then by pulling on the rope we made it tight around the tree above our heads.

Penny laid the flashlight on a tuft of grass so it would shine toward the top of the tree. We walked the rope across the road as far as we could, then began to pull on it and then ease up, pull and ease up, rocking the tree.

Before long, dead branches started falling off the tree as it rocked violently, and we heard several sharp cracks come from the trunk. When I saw it start to topple, I hissed, "Now!" and we pulled on the rope with all our might.

The tree hung in the air at a sharp angle for a moment, then came crashing down right across the road—and we had to leap to get out of the way. Just what we had hoped for.

Penny ran for the flashlight.

"What now?" I said.

"Let's just stay where we are in case he comes," Penny suggested. "He'll never see us back here in the woods."

"Okay," I agreed.

We'd only been standing there about two minutes when we heard the car engine start, and then we saw the car snaking its way out along the dirt road with just its parking lights on.

I figured he'd stop when he got to the tree and try to run on foot. I figured wrong. He must have figured he could go around the tree through the woods, because he backed up and then wheeled the car in our direction. Then he did something worse: He snapped on the headlights.

There we were, the two of us, standing in the bright beams of his headlights. The darkness of the woods had turned as bright as day.

"Run!" I shouted.

We turned and ran, using the car lights to see our way between the trees. We would have made it, too, except that I heard Penny yell and then suddenly she wasn't beside me. I stopped and looked back.

"My ankle!" she shouted. Her leg was tangled in a fallen tree branch. "I can't get it out!" she screamed.

I was down on my knees pulling on her ankle when she screamed again. I looked up and saw Wickner grab her by the arm just as I got her foot free.

I jumped up and ran a few steps away. Wickner and I just stared at each other in the bright car lights.

"Come here, you," he ordered, "if you don't want your little girlfriend to get hurt."

There was a long silence. He must have been squeezing Penny's arm hard. She sounded close to tears when she said, "Do what he says, Chad. He's hurting me."

As I walked toward him, I slipped the flashlight around my back and tucked it into my belt, pulling my sweatshirt over it. I stayed just out of his reach.

"What are you going to do with us?" Penny squeaked.

"I should throttle you both," he said, "for blowing the whistle on me. But do what you're told and I won't hurt you. The two of you are going to be my ticket out of this town, out of this state, maybe out of this country."

He opened the trunk of the car and ordered, "Get in." He yanked Penny's arm upward until she scrambled into the trunk. "You too," he barked at me.

I had no choice. I climbed in beside her.

He slammed the trunk lid down on us.

Pitch dark.

We heard the engine start, then heard him try to drive around the fallen tree. The car bumped and shook. We bounced around inside the trunk as tree branches squealed against the fenders. We were smashing into each other and the spare tire, and we held onto each other to keep from getting hurt. I could feel tools under me.

He stopped and turned the engine off. We heard him get out of the car. It sounded like he was trying to move part of the tree.

Then we heard a *thonk*. It sounded like someone thumping a watermelon with a wooden spoon.

There was silence for a few minutes, then it sounded like he opened the car door for a moment, did something, and then shut it again.

We listened for many minutes after that and heard nothing.

"Should we try to get out of here?" Penny whispered.

"Maybe he's run off on foot," I said.

"How do you open a trunk from the inside?" Penny whispered.

"I don't know, but I have the flashlight."

"You do?" There was a smile in her voice.

In three minutes, with Penny holding the flashlight, I'd found the latch on the trunk lid and figured out how it worked. Using a tire repair tool I pried on the latch. "Push," I whispered. Penny was lying on her back; she pushed the door open slowly with her feet.

We peeked out cautiously. Was he out there waiting for us?

Knot Funny

I stepped out of the trunk as quietly as I could. Penny handed me the flashlight and then she climbed out. But I didn't even need to turn the flashlight on—the car lights were still on. "That's no way to escape," I whispered, "leaving the lights on."

We peeked around from the back of the car, expecting Wickner to pounce on us again any minute. We saw and heard nothing. The silence was broken only by voices drifting from across the creek, one of them Monty Irwin's.

"Look." Penny pointed.

There sat Wickner, leaning against a tree. He looked relaxed and comfortable, as if he were sleeping. "Come on," I whispered. "Even if he chases us, we can outrun him."

"Wait," Penny whispered back. "I think he's unconscious." She took a step or two closer for a better look. "Or dead."

We slowly walked toward him. The headlights still flooded the area with light. "Maybe he's faking," I said. "Don't get too close."

"Look at the rope," Penny said, pointing.

Bill Furrow's rope, at least most of it, had been laid in a neat coil on the ground next to the tree.

I snapped on the flashlight and circled behind the tree Wickner was leaning against. His arms had been pulled back behind the tree, one loop of the rope tied tightly around each wrist, like handcuffs. It looked like whoever tied him up knew what he was doing. Had one of the policemen been here, tied him up, and gone for help?

"He's tied to the tree," I said to Penny—the first words I'd said without whispering in what seemed like hours. "Look—there's blood matted in his hair. I think he's been knocked out."

Just then we heard the police helicopter overhead: *thwop, thwop, thwop.* They must have spotted the car lights. Suddenly gigantic floodlights from the helicopter lit up the clearing even more brightly.

We waved up toward the sky from between the trees.

"THE KIDS ARE OVER HERE," the bullhorn roared from the helicopter. "WE'RE RIGHT OVER THEM." They were signaling Monty Irwin and the others on the far side of the creek.

"ARE YOU KIDS OKAY?"

We nodded and waved. We couldn't shout back. The noise and the wind from the helicopter were like a gigantic storm.

Then the police in the helicopter spotted Wickner. "IS THAT WICKNER?" they asked.

We nodded yes.

"HE LOOKS LIKE HE'S TIED UP. IS HE TIED UP?"

We nodded yes again.

114

"DID YOU KIDS TIE HIM UP?" Before we could answer, we heard a giant laugh from the sky, like the *ho, ho, ho* in Jack in the Beanstalk.

We shook our heads no. No, we didn't tie Wickner up—and we didn't know who did, either.

Seconds later, Monty Irwin walked into the brightly lit clearing, along with another policeman and a policewoman. They all had their guns drawn. When they saw Wickner, the policewoman walked over to him, took a look at the rope that tied his hands, and put her fingers to his neck to feel the pulse. Then she stood up and shouted to be heard over the noise of the helicopter: "He's tied up and seems to be unconscious. Looks like someone whacked him across the head and tied him up."

The policeman pulled a long flashlight from his belt and shined it on the wet earth in front of the car. "Someone dragged him to the tree and tied him up, see?" he shouted, dancing his beam along two parallel tracks that ended up at the heels of Wickner's boots. "All the rest of the tracks seem to have been made by tennis shoes." he said, then shined the flashlight on Penny's tennis shoes—and mine. "I see *three* sets of tracks, though—not counting his boots." He had Penny and I step into the dirt and then examined our tracks "Well, that tells me where two of the sets came from. But what about this one with the fancy pattern? Some kind of tennis shoes, but *whose*?" He focused the beam of the flashlight on a clear print in the dirt—a sneaker print with fancy curls.

Mr. Irwin pulled a radio from his belt and spoke to the helicopter. "Go back and land in the open field," he said, "And call an ambulance. Wickner seems to have sustained some sort of head wound."

They searched the car then. "Wow!" the policewoman shouted from the back seat of the car. "Look at this." We looked over her shoulder as she opened the lid of a suitcase. It was full of money.

"We have him cold," Monty Irwin said. "The EPA will get him for bootlegging toxic waste, and the IRS will nail him, too."

"The IRS—is that the income tax people?" I asked.

"Yep," he answered. "The Internal Revenue Service. You can bet no one has any record of where this suitcase full of money came from—which makes it all undeclared, untaxed earnings. He'll lose all this and be facing big fines as well as jail time."

"We'd better get back to Mrs. Furrow's," Penny said. "She'll want to know what's happened."

"If you want to wade across the creek," Mr. Irwin said, "the police car will give you a ride."

"We can just walk back the way we came," I said.

When we got back, Mrs. Furrow was having a cup of tea. She was rubbing something from a tube onto her right wrist with her left hand, twisting and turning her arm in the air and frowning as if her wrist hurt.

"You're back," she said. "I was worried until the dispatcher told me the helicopter had spotted you. I had no idea where you'd gone."

"Wickner locked us in his car trunk," Penny said.

"So *that's* why you were nowhere—I mean, why the police couldn't find you. What can I get you?" she asked, "Tea? Milk? Cocoa?"

"A cup of cocoa would taste pretty good right now," Penny said.

"Me, too," I said. "Thanks."

"So they caught Wickner, did they?"

"They didn't have to," Penny said. "Someone had whacked him over the head and tied him to a tree with some sort of handcuff knot."

"My goodness," was all Mrs. Furrow said.

Mrs. Furrow got up and went to the refrigerator to get milk. While she was pouring it into a pan by the stove, I noticed she had taken off her Demetrius running shoes. She was wearing ordinary shoes.

I caught Penny's eye and then nodded at Emma's shoes. Penny smiled and nodded. We looked at each other and started to snicker. We tried not to laugh out loud. Pretty soon, though, we were snorting so loud under our breath that Emma noticed.

"Running around in the woods has turned you two characters a little crazier than usual," she said.

Two days later Penny and I got messages at school. We were asked to go to Emma Furrow's as soon as school was out.

When we got there, the first thing we noticed was that Emma's right arm was in a cast. "Hairline fracture," she said. "Must have strained it somehow."

Waiting in Mrs. Furrow's living room was the second surprise—a man. A stranger—at least to us. Mrs.

117

Furrow introduced him as John Walters, from the Environmental Protection Agency office in St. Paul.

"I'm told the two of you are members of Earthkeepers," he said. We nodded. "We certainly do appreciate you Earthkeepers. The more of you the better, I say. I called you here after school to thank you—you and Mrs. Furrow. She tells me that this whole business started because the two of you wanted to recycle some of the scrap in Wickner's Woods."

"That's right," I said.

"Well, you'll be happy to hear that it's *all* going to be recycled. It has to be. Before we can do any cleaning up, we have to go over Wickner's Woods with metal detectors to see just where the barrels are buried. And before we can do that, of course, we have to get all the surface metal gathered up and carted away. We'll have a crew in here in a couple of days to start on that."

"Let *us* do that part," Penny said.

"You? The whole forest?" Mr. Walters acted surprised.

"Of course. We can do it," Penny insisted, "Can't we, Chad? Mr. Kenyon can put one of his trucks over there for us, just like he did here."

"Can we?" I asked Mr. Walters.

He rubbed his chin and thought. "Well," he said slowly, "We'll have to get some meters in there and see if there's anything dangerous in the air or on the ground." Then he smiled. "But if it's safe to walk around in there, I don't see why you can't do the salvaging."

"All right!" Penny grinned, punching a fist into the air.

"Let's run over there right now and take a look," I said to Penny. "There must be a ton of iron and steel lying around."

"While we're there, we'd better check for bugs," Penny said.

"Bugs?" I asked.

"Yeah," she reminded me. "You know. There's a big spider in the creek bed."

"Oh, yeah—big enough to scare a dog," I said.

"Where *is* Wickner's dog?" Mrs. Furrow asked.

"The Humane Society picked him up, I think," Mr. Walters said.

"I'm going down and meet that dog," Emma said. "Maybe I can bring him home and teach him not to be so mean."

Penny and Mrs. Furrow and I touched thumb-prints all around. Then Penny and I ran out the back door and across the road. We stood at the broken-down fence and looked out into Wickner's Woods. It sure seemed a lot different now. A couple of days ago it was scary place, with a mean dog and a meaner farmer. Now I couldn't wait to get back here and do some recycling.

It wasn't a forbidden forest anymore.

DON'T MISS ANY OF CHAD AND PENNY'S ADVENTURES!

The Mystery of the Gun in the Garbage
Book 1 $5.99   0-310-39801-0

While searching for pop cans, Chad and Penny find something else—a gun! And when the gun disappears, the mystery only deepens. Even the police seem to be involved. Who can Chad and Penny trust? There's danger, mystery, and cliff-hanging suspense.

The Mystery of the Headless Tiger
Book 2 $5.99   0-310-39811-8

When Chad and Penny pick up a package thrown from a speeding black Mercedes, they discover more than litter—it's a solid gold statue! But when the Mercedes returns, so does trouble. Before it's over, Chad's mom is kidnapped and the Earthkeepers must find new courage and faith.

The Mystery of the Forbidden Forest
Book 3 $5.99   0-310-39821-5

What's going on in Wickner's Woods? Each night a truck goes in full and comes out empty. What's being left behind? To discover the poisonous truth, Chad and Penny turn to an elderly widow for help. She helps them crack the case and escape with their lives—barely.

The Mystery of the Hidden Archer
Book 4 $5.99   0-310-39831-2

Someone, or some thing, is in the Northwoods near the family cabin. A mysterious archer saves a kidnapped woman, but authorities find only bear tracks. When the bear tracks appear as the Earthkeepers are planting trees, Penny coaxes out the truth, helping the kids right an old wrong, and save a life.